Fields To Boardrooms

From Veteran To Entrepreneur

Table of content

INTRODUCTION
Fields To Boardrooms

The life of a veteran is both challenging and interesting. You serve your country and it's a matter of real pride. You go out to places where very few people would dare to go and face your enemies with courage and bravery. You serve for your nation, your motherland and live the life of a real hero. Hard work and determination backed by proper military training and strict regime forms a part of the daily life of every veteran. But behind all the glory and valor you also know that like any other career eventually it will come to an end. You might retire voluntarily or might face situations which compel you to leave your military service. You might even get injured during any mission or war and find yourself incapable of serving in the military anymore.

At that point in time, many veterans think of starting their own business and become an entrepreneur. If you are one of them and are confused about how to start your own business or company then this is the ideal book for you. It covers in-depth life stories and interviews of eminent veterans like Lena Geronimo, Scott Arias, Mick Dubuis, Crystal Fairley, Greg Jenkins, Haleema Shafeek, James Page, Abdul Baytops, Lee Rainer, William Belknap, Bill Irwin and Ron Eslinger who collectively have more than 100 years of military service. Each share their stories and how all these veteran turn entrepreneurs have become immensely successful in their own field after retirement from military service. You will be immensely surprised to know how these people started from scratch and are now successful business typhoons. You will also come to know how their military background served as a backbone in reshaping their future as successful entrepreneurs.

Now you might be thinking that what is the need for knowing about all these veterans and reading this book but in that case you need to focus on the present scenario and must understand that becoming a successful entrepreneur from a veteran is not an easy task at all and there are several hurdles which you need to overcome in order to become successful in your venture. Nearly half of the veterans of World War II veterans became entrepreneurs but what happened to them? Did all of them become successful? The answer is No. Entrepreneurship is not an easy task for everyone and you need to know the right ways and have the proper traits in you in order to be successful and thus you need to study this book thoroughly in order to know what techniques did the veterans follow in order to become successful businessmen.

The path to become an entrepreneur is getting harder day by day especially for veterans and that's a real big problem not only for the would-be entrepreneurs but also for the military persons who they will hire and for the entire US economy as well. As per Syracuse University's Institute for Veterans and Military Families, a phenomenal 49.7% of the World War II veterans went on to become entrepreneurs or start their own business in the last century. Near about 40% of the veterans involved in the Korean War did the same thing and it created a large number of jobs in the process. But in the present century even if the time span is shorter the rate at which veterans went on to become entrepreneurs or started his or her new venture is substantially low. As per the Bureau of Labor Statistics only 4.5% of the 3.6 million people who have served in the military service till September 11, 2001, have started their own business or have taken the decision to become an independent entrepreneur. If we take all these figures into account then there are roughly 162,000 businesses owned by veterans and since each of them employs about 2 people on an average it creates an estimated job count of 324,000. An average of 200,000 people leaves their military annually and comes within the list of veterans who might become future entrepreneurs. If the present generation would have continued to create the same amount of business just after the Korean War there would have been 1.4 million companies already and a number of job creations would have been approximately 2.8 million. But the problem is that the number is decreasing day by day and lesser veterans are willing to start their own business after retirement from service. They would prefer to get a job and settle down rather than starting their own venture or company. There is a lack of in-service mentorship for current military members and that is what driving the veterans away from starting their own business.

As per Scott Arias, the owner, and president of ACE Consulting, expanding his company was the greatest hurdle faced by him. There are also several reasons for the drop-off like dramatic or drastic changes in the economic scenario and many more but the fact is that the overall rate of startups or new business generation has become drastically low. The days are gone when it was very easy for a returning military veteran to easily move from a platoon to an assembly line and then steadily climb the stairs of management in order to secure all the knowledge and skills to start his own business. The manufacturing jobs do not exist anymore and along with that the bridge to get to the civilian world from the military service has also collapsed.

While still, the veterans have a greater tendency to become entrepreneurs than an average civilian they have very few resources in some areas when compared to their predecessors. For example, while the G.I. bill of this century is considered to be most generous, it does not provide the opportunity to get low-interest loans in order to start a new venture or business when compared to the G.I. bill of World War II. Le Rainer, Founder, and CEO of LR-Associates, LLC mentions that how difficult it was for him to get funds or loan in order to keep his business alive and how the shutdown of President Obama's Administration impacted his business negatively. Many veterans who approached the banks for getting loans for their business got rejected due to the lack of two-year business history and they had to look out for other avenues in order to get funding for their startup business.

Over and above the problem of job creation and declining economic scenario, the recent declining trend in the new veteran business has created a vicious circle for returning military people. The circle goes on like this way, the veterans are opening less number of companies, and this leads to fewer jobs for veterans, and also less number of veteran employers who can create a suitable business and environment which is most comfortable for veterans returning from their military service. This means that there is less number of bosses who understand the difficulty involved in the transformation of the veterans from military service to business or jobs. As per Ewing Marion Kauffman Foundation, in the year 1996 veterans founded almost 12.3% of all the new business that was formed at that time. However, in the year 2004 that number come down to 5.6% and the people who used to be in the armed forces are 30% more likely to hire other veterans as employees than any other normal entrepreneur as per a study conducted by International Franchise Association.

There is still some negativity in the mind of people regarding hiring veterans and they would prefer to hire a normal civilian when compared to a returning military person. There is still this kind of stigma that exists in the mind of people and it affects the employment rate of the veterans after they come back from the armed forces. Moreover, veterans nowadays are less well positioned to do networking which forms a vital aspect for the success of any entrepreneur and they tend to get isolated and lack the outside network which prevents them from becoming a role model and successful businessman. However, the US Small

Business Administration recognizes the importance of the veterans on the American economy and the impact they have on the overall business scenario. As per the latest data collected 1 out of every 10 veterans opt to start his own venture and veteran-owned companies give employment to about 5.8 million individuals. Military service exhibits the highest marginal effect on self-employment and veterans are 45% more likely to get self-employed that a normal person.

Women veterans are staring their own business at a rate that has surpassed the male veterans and civilians and Government have taken special measures to encourage women veteran entrepreneurship like reducing the paperwork required for the formation of a new company and dropping the husband's name from the co-owner title. All these measures have encouraged veterans like Haleema Shafeek to be an example of women empowerment and successfully run her own venture. Moreover, several entrepreneurship programs are now being arranged by the Government and various universities in order to encourage the veterans for staring their own business and giving them the right skills. All these initiative and entrepreneurship programs give the much-needed confidence boost to the veterans which take them one step closer in starting their own business or launching a new company. Further, there are several small business grants available for the veterans that aid them in staring their own business and give them relief from the tension and worry of capital accumulation. Some of the small business grants options for veterans are Veteran Business Outreach Centers, HCC Veteran Entrepreneurship Training (VET) Program, Vocational Rehabilitation and Employment, Grantwatch - Grants for Veterans and many more. The advantage of these grants is that they not only give you funds for starting your business bit also gives you the vital knowledge and skills required to run your business successfully after its launch.

There is a proverb "Every cloud has a silver lining" and the same goes with the veteran-owned business too. Despite all the difficulties of the present scenario, there are some veterans who have struggled their way out to success. This book includes all the success stories of several veterans which you must know in order to venture out yourself for starting your own business. You must know about the techniques and strategies used by them at their difficult time and how they ultimately went on becoming successful. After going through this book you will learn that nothing is easy in life and you need to work in a planned manner and stay focused on your goal in order to achieve it. All the veterans mentioned in this book have undergone military training and strict regime during their service tenure and they learned a lot of things like self-discipline, critical thinking, handling difficult situations and many more. You will get to know how these veterans have utilized their military training and implemented their learning into their own business and made it a success.

CHAPTER ONE

Digital Marketing Strategy
Discussion with Lena Geronimo

The power of your voice can create for you a unique business in life. Lena Geronimo used her voice to market individuals from digital platforms for small businesses and became successful. Lena is a US veteran who transitioned from the military to become a small business owner. She saw the vacuum created within the digital age and turned it into a social media marketing platform, converting individuals into customers for small businesses through a talk show that creates massive service awareness.

Targeting the right audience with the right message is the most effective ad you need to succeed in business. Her online digital company, which she airs on ICON radio FM, specializes in solving marketing challenges for clients. Lena brought together a group of followers and shared them into various business premises. This results in more followers, more listeners, and more clients.

The clicks and proceeds from digital marketing and social media are worth billions of dollars per year. Lena's team don't only talk live on the radio, but they're also equally digital to clients from a platform that holds over 200 million listeners. Lena successfully uses her voice to market small businesses, give those props and recommendations to either improve a bartered business or strengthen some partnerships. Digital marketing can open up new marketing ideas for growth through awareness and build a cultured conscious business to compete with others either in the mass media or the corporate business world.

Lena had a dream from childhood to pursue a digital marketing career either on TV or radio. She can redo a script and match it with the kind of tone that mostly suits it. She handles cases such as alcohol, drugs, prescriptions, and sex with careful marketing techniques, simple and beautiful messages across the society, without messing up those involved.

Lena frowns at the misconception that veterans with PTSD are unable to create a normal impact in American society. As a veteran, entrepreneur and woman with PTSD, Lena has gone through therapies to become a successful small business owner. The military taught her persistence, history, and environmental awareness with the mental capacity to always move forward and fight consistently without looking behind. Veterans looking to do business shouldn't look back; rather, research on your chosen business to know what to achieve and the required teamwork to create a difference. Your business plan should have the entry point, the attack, and the exit points with critical thinking and strategy. This chapter will help you to determine your future with good discipline, multitasking, endurance, long walking energy, and straight schedule to keep your business moving forward.

Thank you so much for joining us today amongst many other areas of specialties. You are considered an expert in your field. Tell us your full name and professional title and about your company.

My name is Lena Geronimo; I am a radio host for talk life radio an online digital company. On ICON radio FM, we specialize in solving digital marketing issues; what we do is, we go in and look for those clients who are in business and actually trying to get to the target customers and help them achieve their goal by marketing their businesses to those individuals in order to get a mass turnout through digital marketing, social media, followers, shares, listeners and things of that sort, so it enhances the digital marketing aspect of any business, small or big.

Briefly describe the outcome that can be achieved by working with you; describe the difference and achieving the outcome you helped them rage can make in their business.

Lena Geronimo: The outcome of course is more followers, more listeners, and more clients. The more individuals know that you're always online, they will be able to click on a link and take a look at your business or the said business that's being marketed and determine right there whether they would consider doing business. Now, when you get some one that actually clicks on your adverts, it's an even bigger benefit to actually market with us because of the simple fact that from those simple clicks from one individual, now we also have the information of that one individual, what they're looking at, what they're searching for, um, when their birthday is, things of that sort about that client that also helps pinpoint, um, you know, the demographic and also, um, the marketing, marketing, I think I said that night. Um, but yeah, business can grow definitely substantially from the, uh, online digital marketing world that we provide with, uh, with talkback radio.

Tell us why you think your business is important. What are the benefits of working with a company like yours?

Lena Geronimo: Well, for one, I think my business is important because there are many small businesses out there that do need the cost effective marketing. And one of the best options and routes that anybody can go with their business is digital marketing. We are talking about a market that is over billions of dollars per year for these clicks and transactions through digital marketing and social media. So my business is important because not only am I talking live on "talk life radio", it is also because we're digital. We are on a platform that also holds over 200 million listeners. And I think the voice is very powerful; so when you team up with a talk show as a small business, not only am I able to give proposals and recommendations to this said small business for either a bartered business or a partnership.

I use talk life radio to market those businesses out there with a cause and those that will definitely do business and take the time out to open their mind to new marketing ideas. And radio is just one of the ways to go. So my business is important. It's the importance of the voice. I think the benefit of working with a company such as ours is growth. I mean that's the only word that really comes to mind; growth and bringing awareness, awareness to WHO's out there in business and what they do what they specialize in. And it goes along the line, even culture conscious businesses and the black owned businesses and you know, targeting those that need to actually get out there in the forefront and not feeling like you have to compete with the mass media or the corporate world. So there is a marketing platform for those people out there.

What stirred you to move in this professional direction? Include a short story about how you caught the bug to do what you do. Describe what drives you and your passion to do what you do and to help others.

Lena Geronimo: My move to this professional direction, it's actually a funny cause so I'm going to start with the story first. So since I was younger, I was very observant of my surroundings and what was being told to me and who was telling it to me. And I noticed that also about mass media. And I knew it was mass media right off the bat, making the connection digitally in my mind with TV, radio and networks and things of that sort. And it always dawned on me like what if they would change this and say this instead or what if they would change this visually and do this instead. And why don't we, you know redo the script for this and kind of tone it down things.

And that's hard but we know that America itself through the years is not like that. There is a lot of alcohol, drugs, prescriptions, sex of course money everywhere. And so the bug for me was to basically get into what I do now is because I want to get back to the basic type of thinking when it comes to marketing. Marketing can be simple, it can be beautiful, but I can also, you know, really mess someone up if they don't have the right marketing. With being able to have a background in radio for so long that is since 2004 and then also a TV background in production and directing it molded those two worlds together to formulate provision by lady, which is also, something I'm working on to get LLC.

So we can also umbrella talk life radio under that and it all goes within a creation, you know, visual creation, audio creation, with the voiceovers and how one business is actually put out there to consumers and what people are taking two more of. There are more and more people that have taken to the social media aspect because mainstream is kind of getting lame with the continuation of what we have been seeing. But we need to let everybody know that there is a different platform that is out there that's growing that also needs people to believe in the vision behind it and then with the event and you know, things of that sort just making sure overall awareness is enhanced with the marketing that we put out there for ourselves. And so the ones that are watching and the ones that are trying to build the legacies. This is why I do what I do. Being able to create voiceovers or beyond a FM production for conference or a business event or even my own networking events.

It all has a cause to bring people together in these main mites that have completely run our country and get down to our real realistic level. This is, this is who we are as small business owners have a hard time creating what they think of their images and with marketing and with talk life radio being able to host and put you out on the spotlight; then to be able to come out to whatever set events or come and review or host an event of yours. It all goes to talk life radio and then television of course takes over with the audio and production aspect of it. So it's all a connection and a building thing. So that's my vision and that's pretty much why I took the professional direction that I have as executive partner at a radio station and also my own creative director role of television and talk life radio.

Typically, how long does it take to recoup an investment in this business?

Lena Geronimo: well, our clients will see a ROI (return on their investment). So I feel the power behind online businesses and online marketing in general is that you can see a return on your investment depending on what the investment is. I would definitely say within the first three months. We are doing an experiment with Griffin studios here in Las Vegas where we created a partnership with them on our marketing skills and they teamed with me doing different shows and broadcast from their studio and for doing that for us, of course I plugged them and make sure that they're getting the right marketing for the barter that we actually agreed to. So with this kind of partnership I would actually have to get back to the return on investment but considering everything is online, it is usually within the first three months that you should see your return on your investment; but that still has to depend on how big your investment is.

What resources have you used or had access to you feel benefited you professionally to grow your business that is exclusive to veterans?

Lena Geronimo: So the only resource that I know that I have had access to that benefited me professionally was the veterans' social connection in Long Beach at the VA hospital in Long Beach, California. It allowed me to Kind of unify with the veteran women that are there in giving clothes away, free clothing, accessories, shoes, hats, scarves like a professional evening outing there are many things that I was able to actually give away and was also able to talk to a lot of veterans about their businesses. What kind of businesses they have and it was just basically a networking. Overall as far as being able to get into the veteran community even more with talk life radio is something I'm looking forward to in the near future and build those resources like get my license from the women veteran business, you know anything that's a women veteran business ownership so I'm still working on all of that.

What misconceptions and fears have you had and have found that fellow veterans have about venturing into this line of entrepreneurship and how did you resolve it?

Lena Geronimo: I think the misconception that veterans with PTSD are not normal parts of society. And that's probably one of the biggest misconceptions of all time because veterans are one of the most brilliantly trained individuals in America today. I mean their integrity standards speak for itself. The military itself, kind of sucks; but the training that is instilled, the consistency that we hold, the readers of skills, and the seeing through mentality is some of the values that I keep and they help me resolve any challenges that I face.

What do you think any veterans should know before deciding to venture into entrepreneurship?

Lena Geronimo: I never really had misconceptions or fears about coming into the line of entrepreneurship that I'm in because I have always loved what I did. It was getting over the misconception of the title that I hold in America. Being a veteran, being a PTSD or survivor, a woman and having to go through therapies and with people thinking you are crazy which is completely far from the truth. So we own businesses, we try to live our lives as normal as possible and I'm living the best normal life as I can especially as a small business owner, woman and veteran business owner and praying to become much bigger. How did I resolve any of these misconceptions and fears? I just kept believing, praying, and eventually overcame whatever anxiety was going on with me; being in uncomfortable situations just to get things done. Anxiety is an uncomfortable feeling and as a host you might think being social is an easy thing, but a lot of sociable people also have social anxiety too. So that's one thing that works against me but I worked through it.

What tools and education did you receive during your military service career that helped you reach your level of success in business today?

Lena Geronimo: I was given an education that definitely made me more aware of my surroundings. It gave me a more move forward mentality where we don't look behind us but we keep moving forward and fighting forward. Which also reminds me of life; you are never supposed to look in the past, but a lot of people do and that's when they get stuck. So with a moving forward mentality I'm just picturing boots, heels hitting the concrete and moving forward.

What do you think any veterans should know before deciding to venture into entrepreneurship?

Lena Geronimo: The ability to definitely get uncomfortable and in such times and situations when you feel the most resistance and you're like I shouldn't worry because whatever

14

is consuming the mind at the time and it weighs confidence and being able to come out of all of that, it's about knowing that you are getting uncomfortable for a reason and you know, it's not a malicious thing to say but getting uncomfortable depends on how you're getting uncomfortable. I'm not saying put yourself in a harmful situation but simply means overcoming those elements like mine; social anxiety or anxiety period and being able to get out of my mind and back into my body to where I am comfortable again. And you got to get uncomfortable in order to be comfortable and then in the end it's like you realize, I can do it right. Cause when you think of it that way, that's what a lot of people with anxiety I think go through.

Secondly persistency, definitely the military gave me those tools as far as the education is concerned. They gave me a vast education of the history of the military because there are different stories about the American history and other histories and histories.

I think any veteran should know research a lot. Research what kind of businesses that are out there so you know the statistics on it, research even the local business administration, the small business administration, there's a lot of research into owning a business and what kind of, things make you look legit. Getting an LLC, do a nonprofit, test your ideas, partner with someone and do an overall and thorough research about your business and even what the benefits are out there, cause there's a lot of benefits as well for veteran business owners and those veterans that want to go into business.

How can you help a veteran who is interested in business and achieve the greatest success?

Lena Geronimo: I can help a veteran achieve great success by marketing them. Being able to be the spokeswoman for a veteran business that has the potential, that has all their marketing needs and now that they're out, we are teaming up and creating different productions around their business and whatever revenue that comes from it that is the greatest success. That will come with how long the partnership is, how open your mind is or creative for their business. And so when you have two business owners, especially veterans that can be open minded to different things, as far as marketing and event production voiceovers, how everything's going to come together makes it more solid and teamwork; that's how they will achieve their greatest success.

Can you share a lesson you learned early in your career as a business leader that you overcame and now makes you the go to person for your prospective clients?

Lena Geronimo: I have different things going on. Artists Vives live is a project where I get artists together and I highlight an artist for two hours live on our digital stream and it's been successful it's on my website and it just continues to grow. As far as networking wise impressions which are going to take over and vent yourself that I originally started for the live broadcasts or small business owners to come out and pretty much promote their business live and it's called impressions because I believe the first impression is the one that matters.

You always want to give people the first impression with your business. I'm not saying for you because usually there are people that will give first impressions really well for their business but these are really quick people. So impression is another project that is still successful. Still looking for a location here in Las Vegas to actually set up shop for that event and of course Bardo marketing services with whoever is generous enough to allow that partnership to happen. So on other accounts, other projects that I'm a part of are pending and this is a creative year for me, so more projects to come.

So some early lessons I learnt in business and radio was to be careful. We've have partners that could use your identity or use your image for their own sake and take a lot of credit for it. And you know, I think just being more aware of who you are getting into business with because it is a contractual thing, whether it's written or verbal.

And so through the downfall of a partnership and radio, a couple of partnerships even in production where a partner did not even show up for the investors meeting or my production company which was the vision productions, which is now" throw version by lady". It's amazing how things come full circle, but you know transitions all the time, that was a partnership with a with a man and then my second one was the radio show with the cousin Chris and that one went under.

And then watching who you give the power to even manage your time; I've even learned that one though was right after the cousin Chris Wood or deal with the partnerships and going to events and raising awareness for different causes. I learnt to trust myself more when it comes to business, when it comes to mind decisions and the things that I have to make, the decisions that I have to make to present myself as well. In that light getting a good team behind you is definitely number one. So I being freshly moved to Vegas has given me a fresh pick of individuals whom I want to work with, where I'm at work and things of that sort.

So I think just with the networking and marketing and stuff that makes me a prospective, go to person, the more I get into the community, the more I know more, I'll be able to network and market with those assets of life, small business, rolling business and community events. So it's just being the social one again and being able to do everything within the law.

What's the most important question veteran veterans should ask themselves as they consider where they are today, where they want to be tomorrow and how they plan to get there?

Every veteran should ask themselves how much passion do you have behind what you're going into, do you find it more of a job or as a hobby, do you love what you do, do you smile when you envision what you are doing. Did you get everything? Did you set a good plan for today? Did you accomplish them? What things did you miss today that you can improve on tomorrow and so like daily goal planning; and with the goal planning, how do they plan on getting there I mean, everybody has to have a plan of action. They need to have a plan, an attack plan; and then of course along the lines later down the road an exit plan too. How much of a critical thinker are you? How are you strategically planning your life around the obligations that need to go into the said business? So it goes with a long list of questions veterans should ask themselves, when you consider where you are today, tomorrow, how you plan on getting there set of course of action.

What three qualities should a veteran reading your chapter consider when choosing to venture into business?

Lena Geronimo: I want veterans to get out of my chapter keeping an open mind, patience and discipline. Being an entrepreneur involves a lot of discipline and multitasking keeping schedules straight and the organization of everything. You are a veteran right and the endurance, cause it does take a lot of energy to come up, create, establish and move a business forward so endurance as well.

Just do it; it will be a long road, go ahead because it will be a rewarding road if you are consistent and persistent so just do it and you never know what you can come up with. My tenacity and will to understand as far as competitors with radio; that's the line, I would have more, I feel I have more compassion, I talk life into things. So it's not just talking about a red table talk but it's also being able to speak life. Actually it is almost like a Grad table talk; it is just like the Polynesian version of Red Table but I gave it a more real, genuine and cultured feel and so I bring a more diverse collection too not only radio, but also marketing.

About Lena Geronimo

Company:

Talk life radio

Who can I help: We help our clients' especially small businesses who seek to grow their companies by marketing their products or services and creating awareness about their brands.

What sets me apart: My team is made up of creative personnel who come up with creative ideas to grow small businesses and bring them prospective clients.

How to get in touch with us:

- Email: lena.geronimo@gmail.com

- Website: www.talkliferadio.com

CHAPTER TWO

Overcoming Personal Barriers + No Holds Barr = To Exceed Professionally

Discussion with Scott Arias

Are you based in Nicholasville, Kentucky, and in need of an excellent Consulting company? Ace Consulting Company, headed by US Navy veteran Scott Arias, got you covered. Ace Consulting is a solutions-based company with a unique selling point to attend to all companies that have skill sets to do contracts. Their team comprises professionals from various backgrounds. With its variety of services ranging from administrative tasks, construction business specification, and the clear outlining of all materials involved in federal contracts, you can be assured to have all your issues on federal construction resolved. Apart from the aforementioned services, Ace Consulting provides plan services, paperwork, bureaucracy, and other preparatory requirements for onsite personnel, including body control managers, safety boxers, superintendents, and project managers to aid good contract execution.

Are you willing to grow your business and make a profit? Do you have a vision which seems impossible? Have you tried it all, and yet you feel like nothing is working? Scott's Company assists in getting lots of veterans to be involved in the construction business. Read on to find out how Scott built his multi-million-dollar company, his challenges and how he overcame them, his strategies and what keeps him going, and his future goals for his business as well as upcoming businesses.

Thank you so much for joining us today. Amongst many other areas of specialty, you are considered an expert in your field. Please tell us your full name, your professional title, and about your company.

My name is Scott Arias, owner and founder of Ace consulting—a solutions-based company that aids companies with skill sets to do their contracts. We equally aid businesses with their construction specifications and outlining all materials involved in federal contracts.

Briefly describe the outcome that can be achieved by working with you.

Scott Arias: One of the major benefits of working with our company is that we are able to perform things that many people take for granted. When they go in and bid a project, we make it easy. We're one of the largest in our field. And to be honest, there are several out there that do pieces and parts of what we do, but we are a solutions-based company. We solve the client's problem, and that's probably the biggest benefit of working with us. We solve the client's problem; we don't just solve an aspect of it—we solve it all.

Tell us why you think your business is important. What are the benefits of working with a company like yours?

Scott Arias: First of all, our company is unique, and that is what makes us important. The standards of project administration and project management are clear, and aside from that, we bring confidence to the general contractors and subcontractors that work on larger projects or federal and commercial projects. We provide the technical expertise that helps companies to expedite their work and ensure that contractors have happy clients so they can retain future work. In other words, we make project management and project administration easy, and that is our vision statement.

What stirred you to move in this professional direction? Include a short story about how you caught the bug to do what you do. Describe what drives you and your passion to do what you do and to help others.

Scott Arias: I was working for a large billion-dollar corporation as an executive at a very young age, and I retired from the Navy early because of the loss of my leg. So, when I retired from the service, I went to work for this $1 billion corporation. But I always wanted the autonomy associated with doing my own thing. The corporate structure kind of held me back a little bit. So, I looked for a niche. And in order to achieve that, and I asked myself, *What do I have that most other people don't have?* And I thought, *Well anybody can be a general contractor, but I understand how project administration and project management works.* So, what I did for nine months was send out emails and call people for several hours a day until I was about to give up when I came across my first client, and in a week, I made $7,000, and we now carry out projects worth millions.

We are a Christian-based company. And the common goal for all of us is to give back and to help grow God's kingdom. And that's what we do. We give 10% of what we make to our local Christian church. What motivates me to do this is, I always had this internal desire to help people, and my organization allows me to do that. We have a way of changing lives, bringing people up, and helping others.

Typically, how long does it take to recoup an investment in this business?

Scott Arias: Well, our investment is fairly minimal compared to many organizations because we are a consultant-based company. The most difficult thing here is the cash flow. So, in terms of the investment of cash flow, if you are going to have half a million dollars going out every month, you've got to think through because you have to put yourself in a cash flow position to do that. That's an ongoing investment. It's not like you can just put a half million dollars in, and then all of a sudden, you are set because, as you grow, you are going to need more money. So, you have to invest more and more. It is really a never-ending process unless you just desire for your organization to be 10 people or a million dollars in revenue, but companies are not like that.

Companies do one of two things: they either grow or they die. They do not stay the same. In order to grow, you have to invest in your company, so it's an ongoing process. And as a continuous process, your kit needs to comprise investing and reinvesting to get your money back. Now, keep in mind that as you invest, you tend to increase your earnings. So, as far as recouping your investments, I say the three-year period is what I think would be acceptable, depending on what business you are in, and obviously, for me, that's what I believe.

What resources have you used, or had access to, that you feel benefited you professionally to grow your business that is exclusive to veterans?

Scott Arias: With regards to the resources that I have had available to me, they are numerous, most of which I acquired from the service. One of the resources I had available to me that actually helped me finish my Ph.D. was the 9/11 GI bill. The bill helped me grow professionally, and it actually helped me pay for my Ph.D. I would say more than anything when you're looking for something to help you professionally growth wise, there are so many benefits because of your veteran status and so many things that you can access, be it a trade school or different professional development programs.

I have seven certifications, and those certifications were paid for from the benefits that I took from the service which have helped me tremendously since I am retired, plus I do not have to worry about medical or some of the other benefits that many people who haven't served worry about. Some stay with jobs just for the benefits, but we receive a lot of those benefits, and being a retired person from the service is huge. And it is a benefit that I think is exclusive to veterans, and it helps take chances that normal people outside the service, normal civilians, will not be able to take. The other one is small business loans that can actually help you grow your business.

What misconceptions and fears have you had and have found that fellow veterans have about venturing into this line of entrepreneurship and how did you resolve it?

Scott Arias: I will have to say that the biggest fear that most people have, especially veterans, is fear of the unknown, to start a business with no certainty. When you're in the service, regardless of what you do, you get paid every two weeks. However, when you work in a small business, you don't have that certainty, and that could scare some people. So, that's a huge fear in many people that I have seen. And it really makes a clear difference between going into business for themselves and having enough to live a better life.

Well, how do you overcome that? What I tell people all the time when we talk about fear is that it can be solved really simply. You have to think about the end goal when you turn 65, and hopefully when you do reach that age, what situation do you want to be in? What would you want to have accomplished? And if you work simply because it brings home enough money for you to get by, you should do something that allows you to have extra free time to accomplish something significant.

What tools and education did you receive during your military service career that helped you reach your level of success in business today?

Scott Arias: The several tools and education I received when I was in the service that helped me succeed are, first of all, the technical skills: Anybody who joins as an enlisted person goes through some technical type of school. I happened to be a CB, so I learned construction. I learned how to be a carpenter and Mason. And through that process, I learned how a building goes together and the technical background that helps me today manage the construction process of a project. So, I understand how long it takes to put up a masonry wall and do rough electrical work, etc. And this really helped me out tremendously.

The leadership training one receives is huge. You don't get that kind of leadership training within the civilian world because they do not teach you how to motivate or manage people. That's something the service puts a lot of effort and time into. So, those tools and the education I received helped me out tremendously.

What do you think any veterans should know before deciding to venture into entrepreneurship?

Scott Arias: Before you decide to venture into a business and be an entrepreneur, you should know that it is going to be a tough road. It is not easy. It is rewarding, though, and your life will be better in the long run, but initially, it's going to be tough. I always tell people who are veterans to think about it this way: it is just like going to boot camp. No matter what branch of service you were, it was tough, but at the end, it was all worth it. And before you decide to do this, you need to understand that there's going to be lots of sacrifices involved. You are not going to have a regular

26

job. You're going to have to make a sacrifice for less money for years, but at the end, you will have a better quality of life, and you will be better off. More importantly, you'll have something to pass to your children or pass on to somebody. It is rewarding but not easy.

How can you help a veteran who is interested in business achieve the greatest success?

Scott Arias: By finding what you are good at. Everybody has something that they are really good at, something that is special to them. You need to find your passion. And once you find that, you do not necessarily worry about the money involved because that passion and competency will ultimately lead to your success. And if you do something you are not passionate about, the chances are you are not going to succeed. And the reason you're not going to succeed is that you do not have that ability to work 14 hours a day because you do not have that passion. Thus, it is important to do something you are passionate about; do something that you are good at and that will be able to grow into something significant.

Can you share an example of a project that you were able to work on and it became successful?

Scott Arias: If I were to give an example of a project that I was able to work on and became successful at, I do not really focus too much on the definition of success because it is very arbitrary. When you have an easy project, it is easy to be successful, and when you have a difficult project, it is tough to be successful. However, success can mean working through a difficult project; even if the outcome is not successful, you have grown from it, and you learned from it. So, talking about my experience, I was the senior project manager in charge of a vehicle maintenance facility, which was difficult with a low bid. So, there we were, about to lose millions of dollars. And we knew that from the very beginning, even before we started construction. I happened to be handed it after it was bided and awarded. It was about four months behind when I came in on a two-year project. This is a five-building complex, with a water tower. And it was difficult because there was so much stuff going on every single day. But we did finish the project on time, and we did make the customer happy. And irrespective of the success, that I feel I still learned a lot about what to do and what not to do.

I was able to learn, which helped me later make accurate wise decisions. One of them is that when you bid a project, you have to be very careful because you could eventually be bankrupt if you make a bad bid or if your bid is not appropriate to cover all your costs. And so, I am very careful about what I do when it comes to estimates in bids because I understand the consequences.

Can you share a lesson you learned early in your career as a business leader that you overcame and now makes you the go-to person for your prospective clients?

Scott Arias: Some of the greatest lessons I learned particularly are from failures. If you wish anything for your children, you should wish that they would go through some failures so they learn from them. As a business leader, every time I tried to do something new, we had some setbacks. I underestimated how long it would take, and it required much more resource; it required a lot more time and effort on my part. Luckily, in my business, it's my time and effort.

The fact is that if you throw something at me, I will figure out how to get it done in one way or the other. So, that is the kind of model and quality that I have because I have taken on things that I am not familiar with but carried on with the projects efficiently. And in the process of doing them, I have learned how to do them and how to beat that. I've learned everything about it. It had to be successful. The first time I ever did a stormwater pollution protection plan, I had never done one before, but it required me to do a lot of research and talk with other people because I wanted to do a good job, as I was being paid for it.

So, that process of going through, studying, and learning helped me a whole lot. That has made me get and keep my clients now, not only because we have done most of those projects, but because we have become technical experts and had to learn everything about what we do. And because our industry is our specialty, people come to us because we have that background that others do not have. Plus, I am a big believer in working through the process, and that is also something that has been able to take us to the top.

What's the most important question veterans should ask themselves as they consider where they are today, where they want to be tomorrow, and how they plan to get there?

Scott Arias: Where they are today or what they need to do tomorrow is not necessarily just the layout and goals. I am all about goal setting, and it is important to establish goals annually, long term and short term goals. But where people mess up is that they have these goals, and a lot of people will say, "Here are my goals; this is what I want to achieve." That is not the issue. Many people write down goals; many people say, "I want to do this, I want to do that." But the difference between people who are successful and unsuccessful is that successful people lay out a plan to get there. Not having a detailed plan is where people fail. So, if you want to be successful, it is pretty simple—have a plan and execute on it; have daily objectives that will lead to your ultimate goal

What three qualities should an event trend reading your chapter consider when choosing to venture into business?

Scott Arias: I would have to say, first of all, you will need to be perseverant. It is very important that you have the ability to push through difficult times because there will be some difficult times. And I think the reason why veterans are successful in business, in general, is that they learn perseverance by going through difficult times while they are in the service. Whether that may be on a combat zone or boot camp, there are numerous different lessons we learned about perseverance and pushing through these difficult moments.

Secondly, there is integrity. There is a lot, especially in my business of construction, of unethical behavior out there, and it is tough. It is easy to compromise your values for the benefit of dollars. However, in the end, it will take you down, or you will be successful in worldly terms and ultimately not successful in the broader terms. Like you know, how your kids look up to you. How do other people see you? Do you want to be known as a person of character and integrity?

And there is courage. The reason I say courage is that you can have perseverance or push through something, you can have integrity doing the right thing, but if you do not have the courage to overcome your fears, then you are never going to make it as a small business owner or an entrepreneur in any way because you are going to have to take some risk. You are going to have to lay everything you worked for down and sacrifice it for something bigger. Plus, if you would want to run a successful business, you are going to have to do things that most people are too afraid to do. So, every veteran needs integrity, perseverance, and courage.

What would you say to a fellow veteran who is seeking to go into business for themselves?

Scott Arias: The number one thing I would say to a fellow veteran going into business is, make sure you are passionate about what you do because if you're passionate about it, you are going to be successful. People who are good at certain things become even better at those things. Apart from that, the other thing I would say is, understand the financial implications of what you are going to do. Cash is king in any business; having working capital is imperative to keep your operation moving forward. Your biggest struggle will probably be to get people to pay or fulfill their commitments financially to you.

So, if you are going to go into business, I would highly advise you to have one other person that you can bring up with you. Not necessarily a partner but another person that you can bring up with you to help you to grow the business because it is tough to do it alone. Having the ability to go to somebody and commiserate with them is very important. Nobody is going to understand what you're going to go through, but it would be much easier if you have someone to share it with.

What sets you and your company apart from your competitors?

Scott Arias: We really do not have competition because we found such a great niche. The fact is that I figured out really quickly that to be successful, you have to find something; that is a niche market. So, what separates us from other people is that we can provide a solutions-based business model for our customers. People want you to solve their problem. There's a lot that goes into that, but what sets us apart as being a solutions-based company is that we are going to help drill your well. And if you look at large corporations, what they try to do is to provide a solution. You have

31

to be able to drive people to accomplish something that brings everybody together.

So, having goals, objectives, and a plan is imperative. And that is what helps separate us from our competitors. Your word is your bond. It's really simple. I learned from being in the services that when you give your word, you keep. So, even if it costs you greatly, personally, professionally, your time, your effort, your money; the fact is, your word is all you have. If you say you are going to go do something, you better go do it. And if you're able to do that, people will run to you to give you their work and their money. They will run to you because they know when you say you are going to do something, you do it.

About Scott Arias

Company:

Ace Consulting

Who can I help? As a solutions-based company, we help clients grow their businesses; we use our technical expertise and skills so as to enable them to satisfy their clients, achieve goals and visions, and make money as well.

What sets me apart: With my experience in the Navy and working with several clients since the start of my company, I have been thrilled with the success because my team endeavors that we provide solutions and business models for our clients. Plus, I have that leadership gift of bringing people together and making them achieve a common goal.

How to get in touch with us:

- Email: sarias@ace-consulting.net

- Website: https://www.ace-consulting.net/

- Social media:

  https://www.linkedin.com/in/scott-arias-b40a3a65/
  https://www.youtube.com/channel/UChlz2lUQ6_wZZf5Ko5Gwa-w
  https://www.instagram.com/aceconsultingky/
  https://www.facebook.com/ACE-Consulting-550366988743724/?view_public_for=550366988743724
  https://www.linkedin.com/company/33190215/admin/

How To Be in a Win-Win Position: Gaining Government Contracts and doing Business with the Government

Conversation with **Mick Dubuis**

Good contracting ability helps keep us safe from present and future risks (including social, financial as well as technological odds). By harnessing contractual alliances, Mick Dubuis developed his iconic personality as a contractual helper. Business owners and entrepreneurs call him "peace of mind" in the seemingly convoluted government contracting process. He is a Service-Disabled U.S. Army veteran and also the founder and CEO of Partners in Energy LLC (PIE). His company is diversified to other industries but primarily focused on the healthcare sector. Some of PIE's business is focused on helping other companies, especially veteran owned companies, to register and do business with the government.

In addition to Program and Project Management, Mick has specialized experience in procurement and contracting activities with expertise in doing business with and within both the state and federal government sectors. The assistance he provides spans the procurement spectrum; from initially registering your business to obtaining a Federal Supply Schedule (FSS), General Services Administration (GSA) or agency specific contract. Capitalizing on his professional experience, he has assisted many entrepreneurs in the growth of their company with the state and federal government, pursuing and eventually securing government contracts. In addition, he is an active federal contractor himself.

Mick uses leadership and responsibility, being two of his primary lessons learned from the military, to guide how he coaches his clients and how he leads his teams. Organization and logical flow are of paramount importance in completing any project. Pursuing business with the government can be looked at from the same perspective because responding to a solicitation issued by a government entity can be a daunting task. He and his team handled the equipment planning, transition planning, service contract planning, and event planning of the first two post-Katrina Hospitals. These projects were crazy complex due to the mixed funding streams involved between the private sector, federal sector and state sectors. His company was also engaged in the activation of the busiest heart and vascular center in California after fourteen years of stale-mates with competing stakeholders. His team is comprised of highly credentialed and experienced individuals that enable PIE to self-execute cost-effective contracts and save millions of dollars for clients. PIE handles activations and deactivations of space, supply chain optimization, government training, contracting, staff augmentation, medical simulation training, leadership training, water safety, government consulting, and the distribution and deployment of equipment, structures, or commodities.

Furthermore, the company writes and implements custom software solutions for clients. Partners in Energy is determined to complete every given job on schedule, no matter the complexity of the contract. Mick can help you to know more about contract performance, compliance, and the dangers of under-bidding agreements with the government. His chapter simplifies the process of doing business with the government.

Thank you so much for joining us today. Amongst many other areas of specialty, you are considered an expert in contractual abilities in the public business environment. Tell us your full name, professional title, and about your company.

Mick Dubuis: My name is Mick Dubuis, and I am the president of Partners In Energy, LLC. My company is a program and project management company. We get involved in a wide arrange of projects. We also distribute equipment and portable structures to meet target project needs. We have particular experience in government acquisitions and procurement processes. Some members of my team and I are former senior-level contracting officers. So, we do understand the administrative process of the solicitation and quotation requirements of government projects. We can help our partners in several activities, like obtaining government contracts, better than they would have otherwise done it upon their own. We are also able to partner with them and manage the deal. Our project management program also comprises invoicing processes and strengthening the customer relationship process, especially after sale and services.

Would you like to mention one big problem you specialize in solving?

Mick Dubuis: Well, one of the big problems that we often encounter with people who engage us is, they want to do business with the federal government, but they do not know where to start. Moreover, they have looked at the system for award management (SAM), and it just seems too confusing for them to register. In that case, we like to remind companies the government, especially the federal government, is the largest consumer of goods and services in the United States. If they are not registered yet in the government award system, they are potentially doing a disservice to their company. It is simple; if they have goods or services, there is a very high chances that the government buys it. So, we happen to be experts at how to register in the system for award management and the complete journey from registration to award of a contract. We walk our clients through the entire process... We explain in layman's terms what each of the federal acquisition regulation clauses or references to the US code means but leave it up to them to do further research if they choose.

Briefly describe the outcome that can be achieved by working with you.

Mick Dubuis: It really depends on what level and which juncture they engage us. If it's registration assistance they want, our customers get benefit from our level of expertise, as we make sure that their registration is active and accurate before we leave them. In addition, we are probably 50% cheaper as compared to our competitors in the country and we take our customers the full distance and not just through part of it. The reason that we are so cheap is that helping people register is just one facet of what we do. We prefer to be a partner with them by providing government contracts in which we offer our services throughout the life cycle of the agreement. By helping companies register and guiding them through the process, it adds to an inventory of companies in which we can partner with on opportunities.

Tell us why you think your business is essential. What are the benefits of working with a company like yours?

Mick Dubuis: Our business is important because the team that I have recruited to help Partners In Energy, LLC, knows the federal procurement process intimately. It enables us to manage the contract management and the contract administration of just about any contract that we could get into, whether it be providing medical simulations or helping to construct a portable building or deploying emergency generators to a disaster area.

Our team understands the process of competition. We know how to fill out all the paperwork and the solicitation. We know how to administer the contract. We know what the government is looking for and how to satisfy their needs. The most important thing is, we understand that it is complicated to write every variable that could ever possibly be in a statement of work (SOW). So, one of the things we pride ourselves on is, we try to give the customer not only what they are specifically asking for but exactly what they intended to ask for.

Typically, how long does it take to recoup an investment in this business?

Mick Dubuis: Firstly, the return on investment (ROI) heavily depends on the type of contract. Supposing they like to be a partner with us and pursue a federal initiative, they see ROI as soon as we get paid. We are probably one of the more competitive price leaders in North America that offer activations and deactivation services at a competitive price. The second thing is, by earning through cost-avoidance due to our turnkey services and a lot of related agencies services, our clients are better able to maintain their initial budget for the project.

What resource have you used or had access to that you feel benefited you professionally to grow your business and is exclusive to veterans?

Mick Dubuis: Obviously the internet is probably the single most useful tool as it provides access to information that is helpful in monitoring opportunities and creating proposals. The internet helped me to grow my business and focus on veterans. I spend a great deal of time doing productive surfing. My personal experiences have also benefited my growth as I was once the head of contracting activity for the fifth largest VA presence in the country at the time. I also try to surround myself with really smart people. Back in the day I was a senior contracting officer and also so was one of the guys that worked with me and help me grow. Having those positions and that training in a prior life provided us with the knowledge of when and how to do business with the federal government.

I'm also big on self-development of my professional and personal skills and I support my team members that do the same. I still occasionally attend some local procurement technical assistance center (PTAC) meetings. PTAC is a wonderful resource for anybody trying to do business with the government. The PTAC teams can help a client walk through the entire process, in addition they will watch opportunities for you and notify you of new solicitations that you might be interested in pursuing.

Another great resource is the Small Business Administration (SBA). Some SBA conferences that I've attended provide a forecast of contracting opportunities which is valuable intel. The SBA is also great for helping you capitalize on any socio-economic advantage that you might have such as being a woman-owned, minority-owned or veteran owned small business. Even as an ex-contracting officer it's important to realize that we still don't know everything. So, attending some SBA conferences did help me because it pointed out the different federal government protocols that I might want to explore for which I was previously unfamiliar. As an example the way NASA does business is completely different than how the Department of Defense (DOD) or Veterans Administration (VA) does business. In NASA, they want you to subcontract first.

What misconceptions and fears have you had (and have found that fellow veterans have) about venturing into this line of entrepreneurship? How did you resolve it?

Mick Dubuis: Great question – one of the major misconceptions that business owners have when submitting a propsal to the government is around total price. Many veterans and other business owners do not understand that they will lose more business by under-bidding than over-bidding. If your proposal is questionably below the standard contract price, the contracting officer will assume that you did not understand the financial complications involved in the contract and throw your project out of the bidding process. Federal contracts have many cost factors, including prevailing wages, insurances, background checks, time value of money, and administrative burdens. Contracting officers expect that your proposal will be reflective of those financial considerations. I'm always reminded of the quizzical looks I used to get back when I was a contracting officer and I would explain to persons that the federal acquisition regulations (FAR) were more designed to stimulate the economy than to find the absolute lowest cost. Contracting Officers have a responsibility to protect the government's interest and ensure that your proposal is fair and reasonable, however they also have a responsibility to protect small businesses from the government by ensuring that specifications are never unnecessarily restrictive, or that the government isn't asking for things outside of the scope. In addition, contracting officers are mandated to set things aside for small businesses when they are below a certain threshold.

As for fears, it's scary trying to fly on your own without a safety net. It also takes some time to get moving and create momentum. Being an entrepreneur is not for everyone but it does have its rewards. If you put your heart and soul into what you believe in, and take advantage of all of the resources available to you including: PTAC, the SBA, the local small business development centers, grant opportunities and other organizations, you can make it work.

What tools and education did you receive during your military service career that helped you to reach your level of success in business today?

Mick Dubuis: Apart from many professional core competencies, the military taught me two things that I practice in my everyday life: it taught me to take on responsibility by trusting others, and it taught me to lead by example. The Army made me a training Non-Commissioned-Officer (NCO) when I was only 19 years old and did not even hold the rank of a NCO. My responsibility was to train others on the operation, set-up and tear-down of a large and expensive piece of equipment. This level of trust and accountability at a very young age taught me that there are personal rewards with assuming responsibility and leading people.

What do you think any veteran should know before they decide to venture into entrepreneurship?

Mick Dubuis: Well, it depends on what you intend on doing. They should make sure to arrange enough resources and build in personal payback during their company building phase. Understanding the financial side of launching is probably one of the most important considerations. Professional connections are often very helpful to facilitate the entire process and act as a sounding board. I personally have several CEOs that advise me. Good business ideas often do not work without a good business plan so creating a good plan is important. PTAC is a great resource for helping you to do that if you don't know how. . They also need to know their market. They need to know what they can offer and how to differentiate themselves from the competition.

It has helped me to be very reflective by analyzing my strengths and weakness. In essence, I sort of do SWOT (strenghts, weaknesses, opportunities and threats) analysis on myself continuously. For example, I was not a big social media user, so I hired people to do that for me. Social media has become ubiquitious in business and you can use the power of social media to obtain work and to acquire skilled people. It's important to understand how scalable you are. To expand your capacity, you have to surround yourself with people that help you grow that capacity. Every veteran must know about their shortcomings and financial limitations and create a plan that will allow them to succeed with the limitations that they have. Understanding your constraints and being able to recognize your opportunities will afford you the best opportunity to succeed.

How can you help a veteran who is interested in business achieve the greatest success?

Mick Dubuis: Well, that's an easy question for us because we get involved from the point that somebody wants to do business with the government and is not currently registered in the system for award management. I even wrote a manual called *Simple Sam*. It kind of walks you through how to register your company (with screenshots). That's step one. Step two is setting yourself up to pursue opportunities. This will involve a variety of activities including marketing, setting up search engines, focusing on areas that you want to pursue and responding timely to solicitations. It helps to do your homework and know your market. For example, in your business plan, do you have a survey of your target market? Do you know who your competitors are so that you can deal with them effectively? While the rest are pricing structure and market positioning strategy. If you access the right websites you can often find the "should-cost" numbers for your proposals. This is what the government is currently paying for a particular good or service.

Government contracts are publicly visible so you can research and get great intel that should help you to formulate your formal proposal. We know where this information is at and can usually help our clients to be competitive.

The quotation and pricing point is significant; it may create a win-win position or may throw your proposal out of the race. We will help you pinpoint how to properly price your financial proposal. Not every opportunity is right to pursue. It's important to understand whether or not you can truly compete based on your company business model and business plan. It doesn't make any sense to pursue a contract that you cannot make any kind of profit on.

Another area that we can help with is that we can negotiate for you once the government engages you to discuss your proposal. If you make it this far, you are in the hunt! Now it's up to you to bring it home. Keep in mind that the government spends a great deal of money to train its contracting officers. Much of this training is around negotiations. Contracting officers know how to analyze your proposal, they know their historical cost and they understand the "should-cost". Trying to negotiate with a federal contracting officer by simply shooting from the hip can cause you to leave a lot of money on the table. My team has had the highest levels of contract negotiation training. We know the processes, the techniques and the tools that the contracting officer is likely to use and we will use the same ones. Generally speaking we can reach an accord pretty quickly. I believe it's important that business owners check their ego at the door when trying to negotiate with the government. There is a systematic process that they will use to negotiate with you. You should understand everything that they understand when you sit down across the table from them. Engaging our company to help you with this can be the smartest investment you might make.

Can you share an example of a project that you were able to work on and it became successful?

Mick Dubuis: We have several projects that were completed successfully under our supervision. One of my favorite projects was opening the first Post-Katrina Hospital. This project was interesting because of its funding complexity, this project had variables that nobody had ever encountered before, at least in this geography. At the start, there was such a mixed bag of funding sources and associated procurement rules for those sources that our first challenge was to create a procurement system that satisfied all funding streams. It included federal dollars, state dollars, and plenty of private sector donations. We had to figure out first how to buy things in a manner that satisfied all oversight entities.

At the initiation stage, we decided to recruit people that had exerience with opening facilities. I needed people familiar with equipment planning, transition planning, project management, human resources, event planning and construction. I then had to train them on how governments work and the processes used in procurement and planning that will satisfy those stakeholders. I also met with the state procurement officer numerous times, including the state attorney, to avoid any future funding mishandling concerns.

Together, we collectively designed a procurement system that satisfied all state, federal, and private sector requirements. So from there, we were able to roll with the planning process. We had a lot of other variables that we had to deal with throughout the project including a tremendous amount of political oversight. When we opened St. Bernard Hospital in Chalmette, Louisiana, it was a pretty happy day. My team had been instrumental in opening a replacement hospital from the ground up. To achieve this we had to resolve all kinds of issues that were not defined. In the end, it was a great achievement, and we repeated this model in New Orleans East. I think it is a remarkable achievement. Now our company can manage emergencies in a better way. There are many stories of successes, and I believe that history speaks for itself. Customers that engage us have never been let down.

Can you share a lesson you learned early in your career as a business leader that you overcame and now makes you the go-to person for your prospective clients?

Mick Dubuis: Probably like most managers I have made a few bad hiring decisions and to make matters worse, there were times that I held on to an employee far longer then I should have in order to try to salvage them. Now I recruit the very best people that I can find and try to pay them super well and treat them in a manner that keeps them in my network. This pays me back with massive dividends because these rock stars help me with complicated projects and the customers easily see the talent that I bring to the table. You cannot avoid the issues arising from hiring the wrong people but I've learned when to cut bait a lot sooner. You have to move on from them and keep marching toward the goals with the best team that you can. When you have the right person at the right place, you do everything and try everything to support and retain them. It ensures better customer engagement and consistency in business growth. I also bought a company in which I did not have industry expertise, nor did I do a proper SWOT analysis. Ironically, by owning that company I gained a skill and certification that to this date has helped me to land my most lucrative contracts. Although I view that business decision as a bad one, it was also an educational one that taught me a lot of things that I'm now capitalizing on.

My combined experiences really help my customers because I'm better able to guide them and keep them from making the mistakes that I made. This helps ensure that we don't burn precious resources on bad pursuits.

Another area that I have overcome to get to where we are today. I had a lot of trouble with finding the right Certified Public Accountant (CPA). I have gone through six of them in the ten years that we have been in business. Today we are in a position in which we retain both a CPA and a tax attorney. It helps me to help the team with a corporate structure, retirement, and other benefits. Make no mistake, without the right tax advice it can be extremely costly. Tax attorneys are expensive, but not as expensive as ignorance.

What's the most important question veterans should ask themselves as they consider where they are today, where they want to be tomorrow, and how they plan to get there?

Mick Dubuis: The most critical question a veteran has to ask themselves is why they are doing this. For example, a married veteran who has children and is taking care of their educational matters, driving them daily from one place to another, has a separate car for his wife, wishes for a lovely home, residing in a nice neighborhood, etc. All of these are motivating factors. Veterans have to understand one thing; they need to do a great job, and it will take some hard work and some sacrifice. Another thing that must be clear is, it is not a military-like job, in which you start your mornings with PT and go for breakfast and then go to your position. Nobody will care what rank you were in the military, nor will everyone treat you with respect. In most cases there is not a formal structure to the way things are done. In private business, you have to maintain discipline out of the box. Your success will depend on your own work-ethic. For my company, I figured out what things I liked doing and what things I didn't like doing. For those things that you do not want to do, you need to hire people to do them or force yourself to have the discipline to get them done. For example, I am not particularly eager to do payroll and taxes, but I had to do it, I had to learn it and I had to manage it. Now we are fortunate enough that I don't have to do it anymore.

Finally, I had to get by on revenue that was substantially less than I was making in the corporate structure when I started my business. However, I viewed it all as just a sacrifice I was enduring for the greater good because I have a long-term goal, I know where I want to be, and what I want to do. So, the most important thing to say to veterans starting their business is: understand the business you are pursuing, understand yourself, follow the discipline you need, and stay on the course because you can do it.

What three qualities should a veteran reading your chapter consider when choosing to venture into business?

Mick Dubuis: I focus on three qualities: be responsible, reliable and professional. Repeat business speaks volumes about the type of company that you are growing. You do not want to be one of the many fly-by-night companies that utilize endless shortcuts to maximize profits to stay in business at the expense of their employees and their quality. Pay the right wages. Carry the right insurances and pay all of your subcontractors as soon as possible. Make sure that you price your proposal so that you can do the job right. If you lose a project because your cost was too high but you know that you priced it correctly and fairly; don't worry about it. You do not want to take on a project in which there is an unrealistic assumption on the cost of quality.

What would you say to a fellow veteran who is seeking to go into business for themselves?

Mick Dubuis: I would encourage them to get their ducks in a row by assessing their strengths; they should look at the opportunity and take advantage of the free entities that will help them with a sound business plan. I would also encourage them to make sure they have enough funds to pursue their business activities. It may take a while for the money to finally start coming in at a faster rate than it is going out.

What sets you and your company apart from your competitors?

Mick Dubuis: Our company is valuable because we provide a program and project management solution under a single umbrella to the government and other clients. We help people that are relatively new or inexperienced in doing business with the government. Most of the companies that we partner with have never done business with the government before. We have still not had a contract within the government in which the contracting officer was not completely happy with us. We follow up on any problems that arises, and we make things simple, accurate, timely, and very responsive. Apart from that, one of the areas that we like to pursue is activating space. Our team has people with expertise in equipment planning and transition planning. We are master schedulers in all tasks and activities. The most competitive edge we have over our competitors is that we do the things that they do not do. For example we think about the ramifications a particular piece of equipment might have to the existing services contracts. We take care of minor issues that are not clearly defined in our scope such as moving a dumpster in a parking lot, creating additional copies of a space plan, creating mock-ups for rooms, etc.

Our company is better because we can help our clients walk through the processes whether it be someone that engaged us to help them sign up for SAM, or someone that engaged us to help activate a space. There is a list of companies out there that do government contracting, and a lot of them do good work, but very few of them do a good job both with the SOW and with standard contract administration and supervision. We do it all and we do it well.

I know a bunch of companies that pursue government contracts for the mere prospect of getting change orders. They know the government can be very dysfunctional. They know that once they venture outside the scope, they can legally request a change order. We practice professionalism, and we do not pursue change-orders that are within the intent of the agreement. Instead, we look at the general scope of the contract and project charter, and we do everything within our power to execute the agreement for the agreed-upon price at the beginning, even if it takes us a little bit longer or we must move a few dumpsters.

Mick Dubuis

Mick Dubuis is the President and Founder of PIE, LLC. He holds a master's degree in Business Administration from Cleveland State University and a bachelor's in management. His professional history includes over 20 years of federal government services, 17 of which were in the procurement field where he ascended to the level of Head of Contracting Activity and Senior Procurement Officer for Northeast HUB of VISN 10 for the Department of Veterans Affairs. He has over 25 years of healthcare experience including holding executive positions for private sector healthcare organizations, as a consultant and as an entrepreneur. Mr. Dubuis has been directly responsible for recruiting and leading the teams that have activated some of the most complex medical facilities in the country including the first two post-Katrina Hospitals, the busiest heart and vascular center in California, and countless federal projects. He now leads teams that are involved in numerous lines of business both within healthcare and in other industries. He has expanded his company into the areas of telemedicine, training, medical simulations, impairment ratings, water safety, equipment and software distribution, software development, supply chain consulting and numerous other areas.

Business Name: Partners in Energy
Website: https://pieadvisors.com

Email: mick@pieadvisors.com

Dedication

This chapter is dedicated to the military service members of this great country. The nation owes you for your service. We hoped that we have properly armed you for your next journey in civilian life. By your willingness to serve and test yourself beyond your limits, you have acquired transferable skills that cannot be taught in any classroom. Good luck!

Acknowledgment

I have been blessed to have had so many mentors in my life. I am surprised in looking back that I learned so much from both good and bad leaders. The good ones taught me what to do and had my back when I made mistakes. The bad ones helped me realize what not to do when I get in their shoes. Special thanks to my wife Tammy who has been by my side through much of my journey. Also to the good ones – thank you Drill Sergeant Neely for whipping me in shape, thank you CPT Ted Kanakis and SFC Lee, thank you Bob Cerza for being my guiding light, Thank you Joe Roberts, Linda Brereton, Sam Wimbish, Marty Traxler, Linda Smith and Bill Montague. You've all contributed to my success.

CHAPTER FOUR

Reduce Overhead and Expand Your Business

Discussion with Crystal Fairley

Sometimes a hobby can be turned into a company or retail outlet to maximize opportunity and increase return on investment. Strategic business planning can also help you to enter the business game without many overhead expenses and the pressures of hiring many employees. Crystal Fairley is a veteran who served in the US Air Force. She and her husband, a US Navy veteran, turned their kitchen lobby into a retail business! Uncle Keith Gourmet Foods, which sells hot sauce and spicy condiments, is a business that started from the kitchen and later expanded into various retail outlets. At times, you don't have to pay somebody to sit there all day long and sell your product and stuff when it can be done from home. You share that cost in business instead of waiting for huge resources to start your company, which may be difficult to achieve.

Crystal Fairley started Uncle Keith's Gourmet Foods with the aim to capture a niche market as *A taste of Southern California.* She succeeded by targeting the companies that manufacture or distribute their products within Southern California. Crystal Fairley's current company goals are to expand their retail outlet online through Walmart and Amazon, become a Corporation, and help veterans or other people to do business through their business in a box concept. One of the core values of the company is that every entrepreneur who has become successful should inspire and think of helping others who are entering into business.

Uncle Keith's Gourmet Foods, located in the US, does not outsource anything overseas. There is an expansion plan this summer to bring another sauce into the market to meet the needs of customers. Grow your business like Crystal Fairley by taking and diverting your income into product development and advertisement.

Crystal Fairley is the Director of Operations, a specialist in business development who has grown her retail outlet steadily for the past three years. She believes that veterans have adequate skills to start their own business and with the right resources and connections, the business can be successful.

Many groups are willing to help through providing business education or business funding. They need to identify these organizations because being in one group leads you into another like a series of opening doors. Most importantly these organizations can provide vendor opportunities to help you reach your target market through hosting events.Crystal Fairley received such assistance from the Rosie Network "Boots to Business Reboot Program."

She enjoys participation in her local Chamber of commerce and desires to make a difference in the community. Her most recent business networking events offered both a silent and live auction which provided funds to support Christmas in Tecate and local disaster relief organizations. As a veteran, you can look up online business platforms or ask questions from SBA to overcome fears about whether your business will work, products will sell, or what products people will buy. Push those fears aside and go forward to put your products on the shelves. Be always willing to take a risk in business if you want to succeed. Think of your business like a planted seed that needs water to germinate and grow. The military taught Crystal Fairley how to structure and organize every business with a core value of integrity; hence the secret of her success. Exclusive female veteran programs like Women Entrepreneurs are good opportunities to network with other veteran opera entrepreneurs. It helps you to hear from veteran business owners who have become successful. Overcome business obstacles by deciding how fast you want to grow and where to put your investments in relation to the ROI. Since business documentation process takes time, in this chapter, Crystal Fairley will make business owners to realize the limited time they have and quickly act to take advantage of opportunities.

Thank you so much for joining us today. Amongst many other areas of specialty, you are considered an authority in your field. Please tell us your full name, your professional title, and about your company.

My name is Crystal Fairley; Director of Operations at Uncle Keith's Gourmet Foods located in San Diego, California. And we provide you with hot sauces for your meals.

Mention one big problem you specialize in solving.

Crystal Fairley: We actually help people have a better meal. We sell hot sauces so people use our products to actually have a more enjoyable experience, whether it's at meals or just a fun experience, because hot sauce is actually very entertaining, especially when you are having challenges, competitions, things of that nature.

Tell us why you think your business is important. What are the benefits of working with a company like yours?

Crystal Fairley: I think our business is important because we actually showcase products from companies located in the Southern California area. So, the benefit of working with our company is that you are actually affecting other small businesses located in the Southern California area.

What stirred you to move in this professional direction Include a short story about how you caught the bug to do what you do? Describe what drives you and your passion to do what you do and to help others.

Crystal Fairley: I got involved in this business because of my husband. He actually caught the hot sauce bug and started with the seed, and then it became a family business. And we used our different roles to be hot sauce innovators. And me being the operations person, I always had a passion for organizing and getting things done. I think because it is a family owned business, we just kind of took the role that fit our personality. I have a history of doing that—management. So, doing the Operations in this business helps me to fulfill that desire to host consumer events or be there in the public eye. Actually, what drives my passion is, I have always had a desire to help other people, whether it is to give them advice to help them grow their business, start a business, or give their confidence a boost. I have always had that desire to help other people.

Typically, how long does it take to recoup an investment in your business?

Crystal Fairley: I think for a company to get an ROI, it depends on what types of investments they are making. If you make investments of products, when the product sells, you are going to receive your return on investment faster than if maybe you joined the Chamber of Commerce because there are certain investments that you are going to make that you will reap financially immediately by the sale of products. So, it depends on the type of investments. Looking back, I probably would have made more investments in the inventory and products rather than investments such as community involvement. Because, now, that takes away from our ROI, and it does extend the time that we will be recouping to actually make a profit. I would encourage people to really look at what they are getting when they want to make an investment and to determine how long. It is not an overnight success, but if you use lean operations and budget wisely, you can actually recoup sooner than later.

What resource have you used or had access to that you feel benefited you professionally to grow your business and is exclusive to veterans?

Crystal Fairley: I did a bunker labs online course. It was really good to get a lot of background knowledge about business. We also participated in the Institute for Veterans and Military Families V-Wise conference. So, there are conferences or educational classes exclusively for veterans at no cost that have really helped; whether it is connecting with other veterans or just giving your confidence a boost by hearing other stories. I have really benefited from those events. That is where I took the boots to business class, and it was really good. Sometimes just networking with other veterans, you will find about programs that they have been involved in, and there are other programs that we have not necessarily been involved with but that we can participate in.

What misconceptions and fears have you had and have found that fellow veterans have about venturing into this line of entrepreneurship and how did you resolve it?

Crystal Fairley: Sometimes you have a fear of being an entrepreneur, and you think, *Okay, I am going to do business, and I am going to go get a job that pays.* And then you think, *No, you know what? I am just going to keep at it.* You may scale back but just keep working on the business because, sometimes, it is easy to just scrap your business and say, "I am going to go and start something else," or "I am going to go and work for somebody else," and it is okay to work for somebody else, but keep the business going. Just scale back and give it time to grow. And I think maybe the misconception is, "I am not where I should be. I want the business to be growing faster." But sometimes, you just need to have patience. Scale back and keep going and see what happens. Trust that your investment is like a seed that is sown, and you know that one day, if you just keep sowing enough seed, you are going to reap a harvest.

What tools and education did you receive during your military service career that helped you reach your level of success in business today?

Crystal Fairley: When it comes to business owning, you have to have a lot of structures, and the military does provide one, whether it is standard operating procedures or just to remind you that as a business owner, you will be more successful if you have a system of organization in place. And that is something that challenges me because I know I need a system in place. Things will run smoothly and work out if I have a system in place, and I think that is something that I got from my military experience.

What do you think any veteran should know before deciding to venture into entrepreneurship?

Crystal Fairley: My husband and I, who are both veterans, started a business. I kind of fell into it; it was part of his passion, and it just became a family business. So, as an entrepreneur, just know that you are starting somewhere. Your role may change. Do not feel that you have to have everything perfect before you start. In other words, you are a master at whatever business you are doing; in other words, I was not a hot sauce guru when I started. I think the idea is to start something and then learn from the mistakes and grow.

And you can always change it, but start somewhere. If your current hobby is hot sauce, then start a hot sauce, something in that current passion. Know that as you go forward, your desires change, and that is okay, but you have to start somewhere. If you are just willing to start somewhere, the process of life will take you to the next challenges.

How can you help a veteran who is interested in business achieve the greatest success?

Crystal Fairley: Well, if you are in the Southern California area, and you have a hot sauce product, we can provide a platform for your product in our store. I think just speaking with somebody and giving feedback on my experience would help someone achieve success. One of the things that I would say to a veteran that is interested in achieving great success is, really take advantage of all the programs that are available, whether it is the SBA, SBDC, etc. There are lots of programs out there, and depending on your product or service, really decide who your target market is, who are you selling to, and get a handle on that. If you know who you are selling to, that will make a difference in your marketing and where you put your product or service.

Can you share an example of a project that you were able to work on and it became successful?

Crystal Fairley: I think one of the projects or the things that we did that became successful was to choose products that we would use for our brand. We looked into products that we can use under the Uncle Keith's branding, and we found a company that we liked. We sampled the products, and then we were able to choose the products that we would actually showcase under our Uncle Keith's brand. This helped because it allowed us to get our brand to market faster, and it saved us on cost

Can you share a lesson you learned early in your career as a business leader that you overcame and now makes you the go-to person for your prospective clients?

Crystal Fairley: I think in the retail industry, with all these businesses going out of business, one of the things that we learned is the lean principle. When you have patience and can wait, it is better than to accumulate debt. I learned that sometimes, slower growth is better than fast growth, depending on your business. You may want to scale back. So, I would say I have learned how to make choices when it comes to debt or inventory—how to make better choices according to the lean principle.

What are the most important question veterans should ask themselves as they consider where they are today, where they want to be tomorrow, and how they plan to get there?

Crystal Fairley: I think one of the things is, "How much of my time am I going to invest in this venture? Am I going to do this full time? Am I going to do this part-time? Is it going to be a side gig?" They all can be a response as to growing a business; it just depends. What do you want to do? Do you want to make this something that consumes all your time? Do you want it to be something that can take part of your time? Really decide how much of your time you want to invest in your business.

What three qualities should a veteran reading your chapter consider when choosing to venture into business?

Crystal Fairley: One is the location. Do you have a location where you can cut the overhead cost? For us, we have that co-working retail space, which really helps us to cut on costs. How much is this going to cost you? Can you afford to do this online or offline? How much will products cost you? Do you have to make a huge investment?

Another thing would be opportunities. What does your market look like? Are you persistent and willing to keep going even when it looks like it is going to take a while for success to be achieved? Are you willing to be persistent with it? Are you willing to be forgiving? People will fail you; are you willing to forgive yourself when you do make mistakes?

Another quality would be faith. Faith in the process; faith in the fact that you made an investment and will reap something. I always think of it as planting a seed. When you plant a seed, you have to have faith that when you water it, it will grow, and you have to have faith in that process.

What would you say to a fellow veteran who is seeking to go into business for themselves?

Crystal Fairley: I would say think it through. If you want to start a business, or if you want to buy a franchise, or if you want to work for somebody, think it through. Ask yourself, "Why do I want to do this?" Is this going to be something that will consume all your time, or is just something you are doing on the side? I would say decide if you are going to be all in. If you want to go into business for yourself, you obviously have to make a way to take care of yourself.

Now, if you are retired from the military, that is one thing. But if you are just getting out, and you have the funding or the finances to survive, think about it. Unless you already have a contract, your finances may suffer. So, I think you have to think it through. Are you going to be dependent on the money that comes from the business? If you are not dependent on the money that comes from the business, I would say start as a hobby and then grow it into a business. It all depends on your situation; think it through and plan it out.

What sets you and your company apart from your competitors?

Crystal Fairley: One of the things that set us apart from other hot sauce stores is just the fact that our overhead is lower. It allows us to have lower price points, and we are a new and growing business. We just have one location, and we have a smaller product line now. Also, as a hot sauce store, we have a taste of southern California. We do have a niche market. We do not sell just any hot sauce; we do focus on hot sauces that are manufactured or distributed from the southern California area. So, that immediately sets us apart from our competitors, and that is pretty much it. When we do grow, there are other options that we can choose from, including location and other things. We do match the manufacturer's prices—we sell at the same price that the manufacturer sells their products.

About Crystal Fairley

Company:

Uncle Keith's Gourmet Foods

Who can I help? As a retail business that deals with food and hot sauce, Uncle Keith's Gourmet foods seeks to enable people to enjoy their meals while creating memories.

What sets me apart: Apart from having a passion for what we do, our foods and hot sauces are quite affordable, and all have a taste of Southern California.

How to get in touch with us:

- Email: admin@unclekeiths.com

- Website: https://www.unclekeiths.com/

- Social media: https://www.facebook.com/Unclekeithsgourmetfoods/

CHAPTER FIVE

March To The Beat Of Leadership Development & Team Building

Conversation with Greg Jenkins

Do you have problems with the way your workers perform and seek to provide value to them? Then you may just have found what you have been looking for. Greg Jenkins Consulting helps organizations build great teams. The CEO, Greg Jenkins, is a US Army veteran and entrepreneur who focuses on leadership and team training. Greg Jenkins Consulting comprises a team of experts teaching diversity, inclusion, and the evolution of business to help leaders, teams, and organizations to fully understand the value of diversity and inclusion in business. In addition, Greg Jenkins Consulting assists organizations to create an inclusive leadership environment for optimum performance. Jenkins' training revolves around strategy development, assessment, facilitation curriculum, training development, executive coaching, and mentorship to help entrepreneurs build profitable businesses. Businesses can benefit from these teachings to enhance team building and higher organizational performance. The training doesn't turn organizations into a diversity company; rather, it helps them to realize the value of diversity and inclusion together toward reaching an organizational peak.

Greg Jenkins Consulting works with veteran entrepreneurs (or veterans who want to start a business) and helps them to make the right decisions. They engage clients with ideas at the planning stage of an organization—whether small, medium, or large business—to improve their business performance with good team structure.

Greg Jenkins teaches clients how to build formidable relationships with their customers and to help them build value, friendship, professionalism, branding, marketing, and communication that can remove anxiety and frustration from business. He helps his clients to understand that inclusive leadership does not only enhance leadership development but also gives them more tools to increase production efficiency and operational cohesion through workshops and courses so as to improve friendly relationships between colleagues and their bosses as well as remove ill-feelings such as rejection, ignorance, and negligence among workers. The expectation of Greg Jenkins Consulting is to increase profits, development, marketing, branding and advertising. Greg Jenkins also offers training, through virtual communication technology which is cost-effective to meet the business goals of clients.

Conversation with Greg Jenkins

Thank you so much for joining us today. Amongst many other areas of specialty, you are considered an expert in your field. Please tell us your full name, your professional title, and about your company.

My name is Greg Jenkins. I am the founder of Greg Jenkins Consulting, and I work primarily in the diversity, inclusion, equity, and leadership space. I am also a veteran of the United States Army. I served for over 28 years as a combat engineer. Though I was a combat engineer, my last 8 plus years in the Army I worked predominantly in the equal opportunity, diversity, and inclusion spaces, as well in the leadership development and teambuilding sectors. I am very happy to be able to share some valuable information with you. I have a master's degree in human resources development, and I officially started my diversity and inclusion career when I attended the Defense Equal Opportunity Management Institute (DEOMI) in 2005.

Mentioned one big problem you specialize in solving and the outcome that can be achieved by working with you.

Greg Jenkins: One big problem that I specialize in solving is organizational challenges with diversity and inclusion, but only when a business is open to growing and developing in that area. Businesses can experience difficulty creating inclusive teams within their workforce. Men and women who go to a workplace to do their jobs, feed their families, and advance their careers want to be recognized and respected. They want to grow, be included, and be part of a team, and we achieve this by developing inclusive leadership environments where people can attain career growth and advancement, thus making organizations more inclusive places to be, which is, of course, one of the biggest benefits of working with me.

We hold talks with organizational executives, providing coaching through trainings, learning, and development discussions. We equally help improve communication amongst colleagues so they can be more effective and efficient at their jobs.

We assess the situation at hand. We design and develop what we think is best based on the analysis of assessments, working in conjunction with key leaders and innovators to ensure that we resolve any issues. Whether it's coaching, mentoring, training, a policy review or a revision to improve communication - whether internal or external - we implement it to improve understanding throughout the entire workforce to make sure that people feel welcomed, respected, valued and included on the team.

Tell us why you think your business is important. What are the benefits of working with a company like yours?

Greg Jenkins: My business is important because it addresses demographics and the challenges of building high performing teams with diverse people and communication challenges that every organization is bound to face. As a country, we have shifting and growing demographics. We have people in positions of leadership who are not comfortable working with different genders, backgrounds, generations, sexual orientations, religions, etc., which are all separate factors that define us as humans. It is important that you partner with us to help you understand the value of diversity and how you as a leader can be inclusive to harness the power of the diversity within your organization.

We bring decades of inclusive leadership experience from the United States military, a fact that I did not fully realize at the beginning of my career. The US military takes men and women from various backgrounds from literally all over the world, puts them on teams, and these teams have to perform at high levels. We have over 28 years of experience, coupled with diversity and inclusive leadership experience combined with years of mentoring and coaching. This depth of knowledge and experience can add value to your organization and your workforce, and I believe this is the greatest benefit of working with the Greg Jenkins Consulting.

What stirred you to move in this professional direction? Describe what drives you and your passion to do what you do and to help others.

Greg Jenkins: In regard to what got me started in this professional direction, I really did not see myself as a United States Army senior leader going into the diversity, inclusion, and equality space. I thought diversity, inclusion, and equality were programs designed for women and minorities, but I discovered how wrong I was during my 16-week course at DEOMI. At DEOMI I learned that these topics was very near and dear to me.

I learned a lot about myself; I learned a lot about others. I learned a lot about how to become a better leader, even though I thought I was one already. The best lessons I received were more about who I am, a better understanding the people around me, and how I could better lead my team and organization.

I knew by the end of the DEOMI course I was going to do this work for the rest of my life. When I successfully completed the course, I was assigned to serve two commanding generals as their equal opportunity, diversity, and inclusion advisor. Those two positions also resulted in my being selected to serve on the Army Diversity Task Force at the Pentagon, where we developed the US Army's first policy on diversity and inclusion. We worked directly with the Chief of Staff and Secretary of the Army. In that effort, our task force evolved into the Army Diversity & Leadership Office, which is still in existence today. Furthermore, I knew as I was approaching my retirement in 2012 that I was going to start a diversity, inclusion and leadership consulting business, I knew this was to be my life's work.

I enjoy working with small, medium, or large companies and their leaders who want to learn more about and understand the power of diversity, and how to help them build more inclusive leaders and workplace environments. I like to help leaders accomplish those tasks, which is what motivated me too. It's my life's calling, and I love it dearly and look forward to opportunities where I am able to apply and share my lessons learned, knowledge, insights and try to help organizations to become better.

Typically, how long does it take to recoup an investment in your business?

Greg Jenkins: Recouping an investment in this business can be immediate, if leaders apply the theory and practices of diversity and inclusion. Organizational leaders that really want to grow and develop can see an immediate impact and changed behavior with their teams. Anybody can manage a group of people, but it takes inclusive leaders to bring out the best in people to accomplish the best. An unhappy environment or workplace results in high levels of turnover, complaints, and reduction of productivity that serves no one well. So, if those things are occurring within your organization you are losing money. But I can teach you how to reduce those occurrences to create a more productive environment where people want to come to your workplace and work as a team because they are empowered and valued. Inclusive leaders demonstrate trust, and trusted leaders grow that trust throughout the team, and leaders and teams that develop that kind of team culture can realize an almost immediate return on investment.

What resources have you used or had access to that you feel benefited you professionally to grow your business and is exclusive to veterans?

Greg Jenkins: First of all, the support and resources I have received from my mentors and coaches have been the most important. I encourage anyone going into business to find mentors and to seek out coaches, these people have helped me the most. Also, as a service-disabled-veteran-owned small-business; The Center for Verification and Evaluation (CVE) certification provides exclusive access to various contracts in the federal and state governments that other businesses do not have. Plus, there is networking; you can be the best at whatever your business is, but if nobody knows who you are, then nobody knows the value that you can provide. I encourage every business to grow every day as much as you can by setting up some kind of strategy through social media, online groups, community organizations, or whatever the case may be. Get out and get involved with people because your networks can be great resources for you as well.

What misconceptions and fears have you had and have found that fellow veterans have about venturing into this line of entrepreneurship and how did you resolve it?

Greg Jenkins: I have witnessed other veterans who've wanted to start a business, but when you ask them "What is the value you provide?" they take a long time to explain and they usually don't know what it is they will do for clients, or at least they can't explain it well. It is a misconception for veterans to think that they will just go into business and start making money right away. You have got to know what your value proposition is. What do you provide to a customer or organization? Are you skilled at providing that value? Plus, you need to be consistent and persistent; work really hard and be passionate about what you do. I am a firm believer that if you are doing what you love to do, you are going to have plenty of energy to carry out your business vision. You really have to go through the process of really knowing your worth and value. It has to be in your heart and mind. You have to understand it for yourself very clearly before you get started.

What tools and education did you receive during your military service career that helped you reach your level of success in business today?

Greg Jenkins: Studying diversity and inclusion really educated me and helped open my mind. But really, the overarching education that I received from my military experience was the best education. The Army values; loyalty, duty, respect, selfless service, honor, integrity, personal courage, along with; learning, persistence, mission accomplishment, not giving up, working hard, being on time, doing what you say you are going to do, etc.

That is just part of being in the military. Every veteran, I think, would understand what perseverance is, and it is what carries you through the bad days, and there are going to be bad days new business leaders, let's be clear about that right now. And if you do not have the discipline in you now, you will not have the persistence to go through the lean days, weeks, months, and years when work is not going well. An added educational advantage was becoming a leader and building and leading teams, being accountable for people and equipment and learning how to better communicate the tasks to my team and making sure they understood the desired outcomes. These are some of the great and life-changing lessons I learned.

What do you think veterans should know before deciding to venture into entrepreneurship?

Greg Jenkins: Every veteran who wants to become an entrepreneur needs to know that the business world is tough. You must know the value of their product or service to your client, and when you know what that value is, find out where you can apply that value and then learn how to market it. Oftentimes veterans approach me and say, "Hey, I want to be an entrepreneur, a small business owner." Yet when I ask them to clarify what their business is about; they do not know how to verbalize it. Veterans need to have a clear vision of the business they want to build. If the veteran entrepreneur can't communicate their own vision, no client or customer will ever understand it, and probably not hire you nor buy from you either.

How can you help a veteran who is interested in business achieve the greatest success?

Greg Jenkins: By helping them understand their value proposition. This is an important place a veteran has to start. Once the value proposition is clear, then they can easily develop their

71

brand, which is paramount in any business. So, you will want to know what your brand is, how you are going to communicate that brand, and the value of your service. How are you going to brand and market your service or product so you can make sales? How are you going to actually find clients? You can just start advertising or hit the streets and knock on a lot of doors. Or maybe what you do is find another organization that does a similar thing that you do and intern with them, volunteer with them, subcontract to them so you learn about the business. It can be very helpful to partner with people that are already successful in that line of business. Another thing is for them to develop their business plan as part of the first step but making sure that their business plan is sound and can be changed as needed.

Can you share an example of a project that you were able to work on and it became successful?

Greg Jenkins: A very successful project that comes to mind is with a company that was in the process of enhancing the development of their organization. What they wanted was to create leaders that would understand and value the diversity of their workforce. This organization wanted its leaders to realize the untapped value of their workforce, to see the intelligent, insightful, and great ideas from their own workforce, which if executed correctly could help make the company run better. If the ideas from the workforce were viable and accepted, they would be able to reduce costs and increase performance levels. It was a real joy to work with that organization because they were dedicated to the inclusion and empowerment of everybody; thus, every team member's input was important, and their ideas were worth considering and implementing. In the end, I felt fulfilled because I was helping the company become better, which made a lot of people feel better about themselves as well. And so, instead of just having a couple of leaders dispersed throughout the company trying to figure out the best practices, lessons learned, and how to improve processes, the entire organization was empowered to do so.

Can you share a lesson you learned early in your career as a business leader that you overcame and now makes you the go-to person for your prospective clients?

Greg Jenkins: I think one of the early lessons I've learned, which has become a great strength is exercising vulnerability. The vulnerability I'm referring to is being fully me, and that has helped me become a much better public speaker, trainer and facilitator. I used to present a façade of military strength, thinking that I would be a more effective consultant. However, it was learning to let go of that façade and becoming more fully me that has allowed me to not only achieve success in business but has allowed me to grow as a person. It goes back to "what's my identify?", and that process may take other veterans along a path of discovering the new and exciting person they can become in the process of starting and running a business.

What's the most important question every veteran should ask themselves as they consider where they are today, where they want to be tomorrow, and how they plan to get there?

Greg Jenkins: I think the first question is, who are you now? What is your purpose, mission, and meaning in life? I think that is really important because in the military we clearly know our positions and tasks, and that is indisputable. But not knowing what you are now, and what you are going to do or what that identity is going to be has be answered by the veteran first. That is something you really have to work on. So, before venturing into business, you need to think through it clearly. Where are you right now? Who are you right now and what's your identity? Where do you want to be tomorrow? How do you want to see that identity grow? These are some of the key factors you need to reflect and work on.

Aside from knowing and working on the aforementioned, you need to be able to plan. You need to ask yourself how you plan on getting there. And if you haven't sat down and laid out some milestones and ways to get there and what resources you are going to need to take you there, you have to figure that out. You have to know your finances, what your debt load looks like. Do you need additional education? What kind of certifications must be required to get to this goal that you have? What is your short, medium, and long-range plan to get to where you want to go so you could expand and build your new business?

What three qualities should a veteran reading your chapter consider when choosing to venture into business?

Greg Jenkins: The first quality I would say is to know your identity. You got to know who you are and where you want to go. And it is important you figure this out because it is difficult and not something you can achieve overnight. It could be a challenging journey, but it is very necessary.

Secondly, you need to be hardworking, building a renowned business is not something that takes a day or two to achieve because the journey can be challenging and frustrating. So, on days when you feel like giving up, your identity plus hard work will be able to keep you going.

And then the third one is, are you willing to develop and learn throughout your life, build networks? You have to be ready to be a lifelong learner so you can continue growing personally and professionally.

What would you say to a fellow veteran who is seeking to go into business for themselves?

Greg Jenkins: A fellow veteran seeking to go into business for themselves should be able to know why they want to do the business and should be ready to do all it takes for them to achieve their goals.

What sets you and your company apart from your competitors?

Greg Jenkins: What sets my company apart from my competitors is my veteran background. It is valuable because I have seen and experienced things a vast portion of American citizens have never had a chance to experience. I have been in diverse organizations, and on high performing teams, and I've traveled to other parts of the world and experienced different people and cultures. I have been in dangerous situations and survived all of it, and I think that is what sets my company apart from my competitors. There are other people in a diversity and inclusion space, but there are very few veterans in that business, and the very few veterans that are in this space do their business a differently than I do. So, I think my experience as a veteran, the way I view diversity and inclusion, and my way of building leadership and highly productive teams is unique because, so far, no one else is doing it exactly the way I do it. And I think that it is evident in the fact that my business has been growing year after year. The other thing I would say is this, I deliver what I promise, providing that value not just because I am a veteran but because I know I still have to deliver. And if you are a veteran going into business, you have to make sure that you are going to deliver on what you say—you need to exercise the integrity you learned as a military member.

About Greg Jenkins

Company: Greg Jenkins Consulting

Who can I help? We help organizations and their leaders who want to build an inclusive higher performing workforce. We help leaders wanting to build better teams. Thus, companies that seek to bring value, fulfillment, and a friendly environment for their workers are our targets.

What sets me apart: Being a veteran of the US Army has given me the exposure in my field of work. I have been able to work with people from different backgrounds as part of a team to achieve our goals. I believe I have the experience to aid any organization that wants to unify the diversity of its workers and make them a more inclusive and productive workforce.

How to get in touch with us:

Email: gregoryjenkinsconsulting@gmail.com

Website: www.gregjenkinsconsulting.com

LinkedIn - https://www.linkedin.com/in/gregjenkinsconsulting/

Twitter - @GregBJenkins

Facebook - https://www.facebook.com/gregjenkinsconsulting/

CHAPTER SIX

Follow Your Passion and Dreams When it Comes to Business

Discussion with Haleema Shafeek

Are you looking for a means to create a healthier work environment for your workers? If so, then Green Office Furniture Solutions, LLC, (GOFS) is your solution. GOFS was founded by U.S. Army veteran Haleema Shafeek and is headquartered in Columbus, Ohio. GOFS has a client base all over the U.S. and provides interior design and commercial furniture & finishes. Haleema was trained as a mechanic for construction equipment repair on diesel engines in the military. She later obtained a degree before starting a business career in interior design.

What makes Haleema's work unique and how did she start her career? After an early medical retirement from the Army, she started physical therapy and ended being accepted into the Department of Veteran Affairs Vocational Rehabilitation Program. This program helped her to work around her physical barriers and attend Sinclair Community College in Dayton, Ohio. Here she would enter to study architecture and later transition her major to interior design. She attracts the artistic side of interior design with deeper initiatives to update, change, and ultimately modify public spaces. By doing this, Haleema makes spaces more superior in beauty with environmental awareness. Her experience comes from both the military and several other commercial furniture exposures she has seen in the course of her various duties.

Haleema started her company, GOFS, LLC in her home office in Hilliard, Ohio and later moved into an office space in

Columbus, Ohio. This move allowed GOFS to add more employees in 2018. She secured her first 7 federal contracts with the U.S. Army at Fort Hood, Texas, in 2008 and 2009, worth $2.5 million. Over a period of 8 to 9 months, she delivered approximately 100 trailers of furniture to their different designated facilities on the base. Haleema was then recognized as one of the top government contractors by Columbus Business First. Additionally, she has done various projects across the U.S. and even had furniture and supplies go out via shipping containment for a project she did as a subcontractor under Lockheed Martin.

Thank you so much for joining us today. Amongst many other areas of specialty, you are considered an expert in your field. Please tell us your full name, your professional title, and about your company.

My name is Haleema Shafeek, and my company is Green Office Furniture Solutions, LLC (GOFS). I have also recently expanded and started a technology company. At the core, we are an interior design-based furniture company that helps companies to reflect their corporate culture and attract talent and achieve optimal functionality through their interior facility design. GOFS provides commercial interior design and space planning. Interior furniture & finishes include anything from artwork, flooring, and other fixtures you would find in a public facility. One of our goals is maintaining sustainable solutions for all our projects. We work on projects across the country, mostly with federal government agencies; however, throughout the year we will also work on state and corporate projects. GOFS has been in business since 2008 and grown to include a supply division. We provide a myriad of items services from basic office supplies that might be a component of the furniture, and initial facility set up. Furthermore, we might offer things like copiers and paper and other things that might be utilized at an established facility to deliver a complete project. We also have integrated some medical and general supplies as well.

In our new technology company, we are looking to provide an array of communication solutions. When you establish a facility in a corporate environment, you typically will need to have workstation (cubicles) to be wired and bring technology into those workstations, through data wiring or some type of fiber optic solution. We have recently found an opportunity to grow in that market based on some of our current existing clientele in the federal market. Having the opportunity to partner and develop with other companies in that industry is very exciting. We are also integrating the technology piece into research and development for the furniture division. Our desire is to help to advance products in this industry that may be cutting edge and lead to helping fuse the industry into futuristic notions of product development. There is a huge opportunity in both the commercial and residential environments solutions to use down the road.

Mention one big problem you specialize in solving and briefly describe the outcome that can be achieved by working with you.

Haleema Shafeek: One big problem that we specialize in solving is making sure that facilities are safe, efficient and healthy. People spend a lot of time in commercial environments, whether it is for work, school, or training for various reasons. In the past, a lot of these facilities utilized products that were not necessarily manufactured or designed in a way that considered safe and/or healthy materials options. Our goal is to incorporate LEED and green certified components into those facilities to create a healthy and environmentally conscious option.

The way a facility's floorplan is designed or planned and utilizes space for efficiency can help to improve coordination of workers and reduce workspace injuries. So, you might have components where people work in separate departments but are set up on opposite sides of the facility. Also, there may be a person sitting in a chair that's not ergonomically supportive and therefore cause them to develop some injuries or become uncomfortable over time if they sit a lot. GOFS creates environments that are safe for employees and builds positive relationships with owners who are conscious of maintaining a safe and healthy environment to reduce workforce injury.

Tell us why you think your business is important. What are the benefits of working with a company like yours?

Haleema Shafeek: We provide commercial grade product solutions that are going to be helpful for that facility and the environment. We work with them to figure out the best way to create workspaces that are conducive to the type of work that they are going to be doing in that area. In addition, we make sure that the furnishings are functional. This means we create an environment that allows employees to flourish, collaborate and can spark innovation because people are comfortable and healthier. These spaces attract the most talented people in their industry and allows companies to retain their most valuable assets; their employees. Another huge benefit to working with GOFS is the assistance resource. We help people come up with interior décor and designs after studying their buildings from a professional point of view. Moreover, you still have the component that some of the chairs and other finishes can be recycled, thus producing a sustainable solution in the office and after the products lifecycle ends.

What stirred you to move in this professional direction? Include a short story about how you caught the bug to do what you do. Describe what drives you and your passion to do what you do and to help others.

Haleema Shafeek: One of the things that made me move into this profession was my passion for architecture and art. I was enrolled in an architecture and design program incorporated in the high school that I attended back in Dayton, Ohio. I always had a desire to work in either architecture, design, or something along those lines. Although I went into the military and did something different, when I came out, I pursued architecture again. Later, I decided what I really wanted was to focus on **interior** design. Part of the reason my focus became sustainable aspects of design was years of working in the industry and realizing there were a lot of practices (manufacturing, shipping, or installing products) that I wanted to improve.

I first started considering sustainability when I was working for a small furniture remanufacturing company located in Worthington, Ohio. Many, companies would go out of business or downsize and would have all this furniture leftover (workstations cubicles, chairs, and file cabinets) that were typically shipped to landfills. These products, which are made of mostly metal, fabric and other toxic materials have recyclable parts, but in a landfill, can often sit there for years and not go anywhere. The company in Worthington would go in and remove those products out of the downsizing or closing office and then re-manufacture it. They would make it look new and beautiful then resell it. I found this experience to be quite interesting and considerate of the environment. This made me focused and study more on what this "Green" "Sustainable" movement was about. The more research I did, the more I realized this was something I wanted to be a part of.

Typically, how long does it take to recoup an investment in your business?

Haleema Shafeek: Depending on the project, it can vary. Our work takes time, as almost everything we do is custom made-to-order. So, from the time we receive an approved project, it might take a few weeks to finalize finishes before we even place an order with the manufacturer. Once the order is processed and in production, it can take three to six weeks to deliver. However, depending on the type of project and if custom finishes are being used, production time could be longer and shipping time varies as products go to the warehouse. Again, based on the size of the project at the site, installation could take a day or more to complete. We also work on construction projects and these can be delayed based on any delays in the construction process.

What resource have you used or had access to that you feel benefited you professionally to grow your business and is exclusive to veterans?

Haleema Shafeek: The key benefit that I have been able to have as a veteran owned business is my CVE certification from the Department of Veterans Affairs. By being certified, my clients do not have any concerns because they know they are doing business with a company that the VA has vetted and confirmed is truly veteran owned. Being certified has been a huge benefit for us and has created a lot of opportunity to help us grow. Having our GSA/FSS schedules has also been a huge benefit. We have been able to do work with several local and national federal agencies that have mandated goals to do business with Veteran and Service-Disabled Veteran Businesses and are required to utilize GSA/FSS schedules for purchasing.

Other very helpful organizations for me have been the SBA (Small Business Administration, & PTAC. Another organization called Bunker Labs that is growing across the country has been helpful in positioning me to assist other aspiring veteran entrepreneurs. Bunker Labs came to Columbus a few years ago with a mission to assist veterans and veteran's family members who are interested in starting a business. This organization can be helpful to our growth with the new technology division, as we partner with other veteran owned businesses.

What misconceptions and fears have you had and have found that fellow veterans have about venturing into this line of entrepreneurship and how did you resolve it?

Haleema Shafeek: "Access to capital is easy" is one of the misconceptions and "Growing a business from the ground level up (Bootstrapping)" is one of the fears that I've had or found that fellow veterans have about venturing into entrepreneurship. When I started the business in 2008, the economy was not very good, so it was a huge concern for me, especially trying to get funding for the business; banks were not lending, and a lot was happening financially. I sat with government contracts in hand, wondering where to get two and a half million dollars so this business can survive and continue to do what we do.

Additionally, how are we going to continue to grow and get funding? I will say that that is one thing a lot of people do not think about. One of the ways that I resolved this was by benefitting from an escrow funding account. I think some people do not realize you can open the door to conversation and requests to your vendors as part of your relationship with your them so they can understand your small business. It also helped tremendously that there are federal government agencies that will pay small businesses in 14 days (in most cases) which helps to create a positive cash flow. Unfortunately, I have found that most people are not aware of this or have not identified or pursued opportunities with those agencies.

What tools and education did you receive during your military service career that helped you reach your level of success in business today?

Haleema Shafeek: One of the tools and education that I received during military service that helped me reach this level of success was being trained to do construction equipment repair. This was a distant thing from doing commercial interior design and providing a service and product for commercial facilities. But what I did take away from the training in general, from basic training to overall training in the military, was teamwork. I learned to either develop or work within a team and focus on our goal to achieve whatever we must by any means necessary. Staying power is another thing that I learned from my military service. It is important to understand that you have a particular outcome that you want to achieve. You are going to constantly run into scenarios or situations that are new, different, and challenging. Having staying power will help you find a solution when there does not appear to be one.

Adapting is important as well. The world around us is changing drastically with all the new technology impacting our world. If you are not capable of adapting and keeping up with the technology changes, it could mean that your business is no longer ready for business. You must be ready for change at any given moment. This business can be extremely fluid at times.

What do you think any veterans should know before deciding to venture into entrepreneurship?

Haleema Shafeek: First, sleep is not a mission. You juggle your day or your responsibilities throughout the day. Whether it is family, life in general, health-related, or something that you must achieve for the business, you will manage many things. Being an entrepreneur, you should do something that you are passionate about. That passion is what is going to drive you through some of those long, lonely nights when everyone else around you is asleep, yet you are awake working.

Also, make sure that you are maintaining a healthy lifestyle so that you can stay well enough to function and nurture your business. You will need to achieve a whole life balance with family and friends. Those commitments may have to change slightly while you are pursuing entrepreneurship. Your family may not always understand why you travel and do things they are not necessarily a part of. However, these aspects are essential because it is a part of the work you do as an entrepreneur. You are going to have to spend a lot of time promoting yourself and your company which can take you away from the things that you may be used to. Networking and building relationships is critical. Thus, as an aspiring entrepreneur, you will need to be flexible.

How can you help a veteran who is interested in business achieve the greatest success?

Haleema Shafeek: Actually, I can do this by working with them one on one and discussing business growth and opportunities that are bigger or beyond what they are doing today. A lot of veterans that are entrepreneurs, start a business, and say, "I just want to get things started and do a little bit here and there". This is not the case because you will really need to review and carve out a market that is going to benefit you in order to be successful at a certain level that is above where you are thinking. I would also inform them about programs I completed like the SBA's Emerging Leaders, Goldman Sachs 10,000 Small Businesses, MIT Sloan Executive business courses and others that are available like Bunker Labs programs for Veteran Entrepreneurs and other executive business programs that are free of charge for qualifying entrepreneurs. These resources will help you continue growth and be sustainable as a business.

Another thing I would help them with is finding out more about federal and other government project opportunities in their market. Being able to navigate through that space can have a great impact on their success.

Can you share an example of a project that you were able to work on and it became successful?

Haleema Shafeek: Years back, right after I started the business there was a project that I was fortunate to work on. It was a group of contracts for furniture consisting more than 100 trailers of furniture going to Ft. Hood, Texas. There were several delivery points on the base, as well as product coming from multiple furniture vendors. There was a mixture of types of product from desks, chairs, workstations, conference and storage. At the time, I was expecting my second child, so I decided to put a project manager on the ground for a few weeks to work out the details with each unit. From there, I worked with my team to finalize the orders and the logistics of the deliveries. We managed all the order details, confirmed items, planned for shipping, installations, and managed final delivery needs. During one of the weekly deliveries, I flew down to meet with the client and our installers for a couple of days. We managed to deliver and install everything in a few months and to the customer's satisfaction.

I worked also worked on a construction project for the U.S. Army Corp of Engineers where we provided product for a Coast Guard boat repair facility in Cleveland, Ohio. We worked with the architect to finalize furniture specifications and attended virtual and in person project meetings during construction for their new facility. This project had a LEED Silver goal, therefore we had to select products that would provide LEED credits for the client and prepare supporting documents for the project manager. We provided workstations, storage racks, recycling containers, seating and other products for the facility. Our installers had to work within parameters of how to properly discard of any packaging or waste in recycling areas in order to maintain credits for the LEED Silver goal. This project was also a success.

Can you share a lesson you learned early in your career as a business leader that you overcame and now makes you the go-to person for your prospective clients?

Haleema Shafeek: One lesson that I learned early in my career was that I had to learn and understand my client's needs. Overcoming this obstacle propelled me into becoming a successful business leader and a better person for my clients. While knowing that my client could be local or anywhere else in the U.S., I had to make sure that I developed the relationships that were necessary to service that client no matter where they were located.

What is the most important question veteran veterans should ask themselves as they consider where they are today, where they want to be tomorrow, and how they plan to get there?

Haleema Shafeek: I think that some of the most important things veterans should ask themselves as they consider where they are today, is where do they want to be tomorrow is, "how do they plan on getting there", and "are they flexible"? Also, "are they ready for change and for whatever is to come; the unknown"? These questions are important because you are going to sit down and do some planning, maybe come up with a business plan and idea of what you are going to do. How are you going to do it, and how are you going to achieve those things? It takes you being able to say, "No matter what is going to be thrown at me today, that I did not expect, I am still going to accomplish my goals."

What three qualities should a veteran reading your chapter consider when choosing to venture into business?

Haleema Shafeek: First, are you self-driven? Can you truly say that you are the type of person to get up knowing that you need to achieve or make things happen? You need to understand that you are going to have a lot of variables that are unknown and make some new discoveries that need to be addressed. You really need to be the self-driver before you choose to venture into business. You need confidence and cannot be afraid to ask questions, ask for what you want and locate resources and be ready to look beyond your known network of people. Utilize the resources whether an organization or training. Even when you think you know what you need to know you might find that you learn something new.

Second, be ready to promote your business. You must embrace to the fact that you are going to be pursuing business with people who don't know you and your business. Therefore, you need to market yourself, market your company, and make sure that when you leave that client, people know who you are, they know your business, and they have a clear understanding of your product, services, or goods and how to do business with you.

And third quality is that you really need to be able to consider whether you might be able to achieve life balance in owning a business and make this a priority. I mentioned this because I think it is a key component. If you are not taking care of yourself, you are not going to be able to have a successful business because if you are ill or sick, the business will be affected as well. So, health and well-being are very important when you're choosing to be an entrepreneur.

What would you say to a fellow veteran who is seeking to go into business for themselves?

Haleema Shafeek: In the military, you received training which average citizens are sometimes not capable of receiving. If you are interested in becoming an entrepreneur to achieve a goal of advancing your career or for life balance, there are certain tools that you need. If those tools include more education, then get online and research. Find your way to an extended executive learning platform that can give you the knowledge and information that you are going to need to be successful as a business owner in that career.

There are tons of resources out there for veterans. Take advantage of them. Sometimes, as veterans, we have a lot of pride, and we do not want to ask for things, and we feel like we will just figure it out. Do not be afraid to ask questions, ask for help, or look in places that are untraditional for answers. Open your mind to new ideas, look at new technology, and become familiar with them, and embrace them. Try to find a way to incorporate it and learn as much as you can on your own as well with help from others too. This can help you advance your entrepreneurial career.

What sets to you and your company apart from your competitors?

Haleema Shafeek: Traditionally, the construction and commercial furniture industry is owned and dominated by males. What I mean by that is, there are not many female interior designers out there who are independent and working primarily on the federal opportunities (most work in the corporate facility market). I am one of the few female minorities and veterans that owns a company in this space. I provide design service, products, and solutions on a national level with federal agencies. This combination is a little bit of an anomaly in this industry. It has been a male-driven market for many years, but we have been successful and this kind of sets us apart. There are other women owned companies in this industry, but they typically are not actually veterans themselves. We also have direct relationships with our vendors, which a lot of small companies do not have established.

About Haleema Shafeek

Company:

Green Office Furniture Solutions, LLC, (aka GOFS Corporate Interiors, ltd)
Dba GOFS Supply & GOFS Tech, ltd.

Who can I help?

We help clients who are willing to create a work-friendly and healthy working environment for their employees and attract talent through an accurate depiction of their corporate culture using our furniture and designs.

What sets me apart?

I offer my clients first-class durable furnishings which will provide a comfortable working environment for the staffs of the organization. Apart from that, I communicate and work directly with my clients, creating cordial relationships to better understand their needs.

How to get in touch with us:

- Email: haleema@gofsllc.com
- Phone: (614) 452-7222
- Website: www.GOFSLLC.com
- **Facebook Link**

  https://www.facebook.com/haleema.shafeek
- https://www.facebook.com/GOFSLLC
- **LinkedIn Link** https://www.linkedin.com/in/gofsllc/

Acknowledgments

I would like to thank God first for giving me faith, love, strength, wisdom and determination in the face of adversity. I want to thank my loving and supportive family, children Antonio Marrow II and Nia Nation, parents Naeema and Hameed II. Siblings; Sultina, Hasina, Hameed III, Qamar, Shakir, LeAsiah, Princess, Olajuwon, Aunt June, Cousins Jamina & Angela Petty, my magnificent nieces & nephews. Special friends LaTawnia and Kenneth Wallace (wouldn't be here without you), Regina Cole, Tondalaya & George Trammell, Stacy L and dearest friend Jay Thompson (thanks for golf and good times).

CHAPTER SEVEN

Fail Forward" How to succeed by overcoming failures!

Discussion with Jimi Page

There are no limitations when it comes to life or business neither should you be scared of failures because they help you grow. Are you scared of starting your business because you feel you do not have the required education or too old to study and start your business? Jimi Page beats this notion; the story of Jimi is an indication that there is no limitation to success as long as you are committed and willing to achieve your vision and goals. Many people feel that because they are not educated; they cannot start or run a successful business. Jimi started and managed his business before pursuing his degree; even though he was a sixth grade dropout he still conquered all educational odds to earn a bachelor's degree and will soon be earning his professorship. Despite the challenges one faces with adult education, making excuses will never lead you to success but hard work and determination will. Today Jimi's company which he started 30 years ago is worth $5 million (dollars). His goal is to run an office equipment company similar to Amazon in terms of solutions, services and deliveries. He runs a non-profit organization called "Cadence" which is aimed at helping veterans. He also helps the community through teaching and training people in mathematics and cybersecurity. Aside from this Jimi plans to build a charter school that will teach leadership and development. He urges everyone who reads this to see any failure as a way forward and that life is a journey and not a race and even if you fail, fail forward.

Thank you so much for joining us today amongst many other areas of specialty. You are considered an expert in your field. Please tell us your full name, your professional title, and about your company.

My name is Jimi Page, the president and CEO of Page global Inc. We are a document management and office equipment located in the 50 states across the country including Guam, Puerto-rico, Alaska and Hawaii with headquarters in Washington Dc. We also offer cyber related programs; we do business with the government and the public in document management office equipment, and have well done various jobs for the Federal Government, Justice Department, Department of Agriculture, and Homeland security. I have been in business for almost 40 years; established my company on the 14th of February 1991 after purchasing a 10 year old business in that started in 1981.

So as a business owner, what are your short term goals for the business and what are your long-term goals?

Jimi Page: Our short term goal is to provide savings for our clients, to always increase the awareness that our customers are looking for through our support and assistance every day and staying abreast of the latest technology while our long term goal is to be able to provide solutions, deliveries, service similar to amazon.

What stirred you to move in this professional direction Include a short story about how you caught the bug to do what you do?

Jimi Page: I joined the United States Navy in 1991 with the Yeoman being my specialty. I started at the lowest rank, which is a seaman recruit. I stayed in this position for eight years. We started the first version of the desert storm; we stayed in the gulf for two years which was considered Iraq and we called it the gonzo station when we had the hostage crisis, we would actually pronounce as being at war inside the golf area. Gonzo was named after the gods oak character on the moppets and that was our logo too but it was, it was called operation desert storms and that is where the helicopters shot off of our plane to go rescue the hostages. There was a failed attempt and we were there at once.

Jimi Page: As a matter of fact, I was a high school dropout at sixth grade level. I was going into the military on a buddy program with an individual named jade James Evans. We both went to the recruiter and told the recruiter we wanted to come on a buddy plan. We actually wanted to go to Annapolis to be officers, which shows how naive we were, we didn't even realize that you needed a high school education. The interesting thing was the recruiter didn't laugh or regarded us as some bunch of psychos. He simply told us "you will not be able to go into the officers program because you need a high school degree, but you could come in because you need a college degree, you could come in to the navy if you got either a high school diploma or ged and I can tell you several places that you can go to get your ged". So he gave us three locations and we decided to take his offer of going to take out the ttd at a school called Evander Childs located at the Bronx in New York so I and James Evans did go and took out ged tests and when we got the results back a week later, found out that we both failed. However, I don't know what he scored, but I failed it by one point. You needed a 177 score and I got 176 so we had two weeks to go back and take it.

We were both rascals at that age, so we would kind of hang out on the block. It was a local bar that we used to go; doing things that rascals are supposed to do. So two weeks later I went to James' house and said "hey, we got to go sign up so we can go take the test again" and he said, "I'm going on the block, which meant he wanted to go be a rascal". And I told him, you know what, I'm going to go take the test and he said you should come with me. I took the test and made it back home. Two weeks later, my mother called me saying she has got some great news for me. You passed the test by one point. So I was 16 at the time. So she signed me up not wanting to delay my program. So actually I went into the navy at 16 years of age, didn't get assigned to a duty station until my 17th birthday, which is February the 14th when I was out, I came home for boot camp for two weeks; and later my best friend James Evans was shot several times and killed by the rascals we used to hang out with and I am sure I would've been with him and the rest changed my life.

What tools and education did you receive during your military service career that helps you reach your level of success in business today?

Jimi Page: Oh, actually I am currently in school now. I decided to go back when I went into the military and I signed up the school. When I was in school to get my engineering degree, that is when I met my wife and she told me that we were having a child. This was my second child out of wedlock and I decided I didn't want to go down his path. So we got married; I met her in the navy and decided to make a family of it. And I had dropped out of school but it wasn't until actually two years ago that I got focused on going to school and I have been schooled, now looking at graduating in March with my associates and I was told that there's a good chance right now for me to get an honorary degree from Georgetown university because of the 30 years of business success and the things I've been doing in the community. Going back to school has given me a whole new appreciation of what education can do in a person's life, absolutely never realized that before.

I did not have a mathematical foundation schools just pass me by because I was able to smile and I guess I look pretty educated but didn't know what two plus two was. Well that was before our standardized testing requirements; so schools were more liberal. So when I actually decided to get serious about school, they told me that I had to start at a premed. So there were nine levels of this math course that I had to take at nova. Normally it takes three years to go through but my situation needed nine years but was able to do it in two years. And of course I got kicked back from my wife because she said; why can't you just get a liberal arts degree? You only need five; why do you have to be so hard on yourself? So I said honey, I've been a business owner for over 25 years why would I want to get a liberal arts degree? I tried to speed it up because I got a little anxious and I finally graduated last semester during last summer after studying pre- math, which was algebra. So I did my entire nine unit, to that scored a 98 on my algebra final algebra test, so I thought I could graduate sooner if I took a 16 week course or eight week course in pre-calculus and calculus.

So when I took my first test, I scored an 11; my second test I scored at 36, but I never got the results of my final. So when he gave me my final, I scored a 78, so I told him I scored a 78 in calculus and he said, yeah but your grades didn't add up to what I would be able to pass you up. So in my mind I celebrated it because here is a child who dropped out of school without a math foundation. I still continued with the calculus course because I had already signed up and paid for it through the military. She said you can still take an eight week class in calculus if you want or you can drop out but I'm not going to make you not take it. So I told her, you know, I'll take calculus still. So I'm happy to say that I did take like eight week calculus course and I was able to graduate out of that with a C and now I'm enrolled in my final class before I graduated in March with the same professor who gave me an F, so my goal is to get an A and absolutely why not and would be proud to finally graduate and share my story someday.

Because the journey of being in business for 30 years being a dropout and being able to build a successful business to almost $5 million dollars and have a company that is servicing the nation, and also being able to give back my community and being able to teach and train others to do a math and then cyber security. And along with having five years of a successful marriage for over 30 years, 33 years to be exact and having five children that have college degrees, gets me going back to build a charter school, teaching leadership and development with a focus on math. What took me back to go back to school was that if I have enough money to build a charter school, but I couldn't teach there because I'm not an educated man standard. So my goal is to go back of course and get the education so that so I can also be a professor and teach at the school. I feel elated because it's not as easy and people don't realize that it's at 17, 18, 19, and 20 or generally in your early twenties with no other commitments or distractions that you easily get your education. But at our adulthood; we are face the need to support our families, work and still have to support our children, attend events and activities and everything else, whether they're young or old. And it becomes a very hard struggle to balance that education along with our professional careers no matter what it is, whether it's working at a fast food joint or running a business. So

I take it that your business then supports continuing education for employees.

We have hired so military veterans and we've started a nonprofit called cadence. The goal is keeping drum beats empowered now for service members everywhere. So it's kind of a playoff you know, we had military always marching to a different cadence, different drummer. So our objective is to be able to have the drum beats of nationalities people.

What do you think any veterans should know before deciding to venture into entrepreneurship?

Jimi Page: Failure is an opportunity to learn and being in computers; I find it interesting that computers we designed today are designed to succeed. Every computer's intention is to successfully solve your problems. However it takes human beings to create problems and it seems like there is always a job for problems since we are always building computers to solve them and we'll never be out maneuvered by computers because it seems as though we always have a plethora of problems to solve. So if we get on in front of the problems and the only way you can get in front of the problems is by failing but you can create a society in the future that computers would help address because they're addressing the current problems. They afford us the opportunity of more work and job opportunities. But actually it's our business and ability to think outside the box.

Can you share a lesson you learned early in your career as a business leader that you overcame and now makes you the go to person for your perspective clients?

Jimi Page: I will share this story with you; I was having a little difficulty in my marriage. I was having a little bit difficulty connecting with my children. I'm a whistler; my dad used to tell me you know what the secret or whistling is he can't whistle and cry at the same time so always keep your head up and people would wonder what you are up to. And it's always a positive, not a negative; not only does it lift your spirit but lifts other people's spirits up around. So I've always been a whistler with my back up against the wall. So he's talking about his ship and how he commanded a seven fleet, which is a logic unit and I overheard him came around the corner. He was getting fitted for a suit and when seeing that I was in a suit and said, hey see you are in a suit, what do you do?

So I said I own a business. He said, wow. He said that's great; he says I'm looking for tie to go with the suits. I said well, if it's a job interview, you wouldn't go with a red top. So he said, you know what that's a good idea; I was thinking about that too. So he asked me what I did. I told him what I did and he told me what he did. He was a commander of a captain battleship group; so he said he is looking for a job. So when I told him that I was having a little bit of trouble you know, with my marriage and my children, and it was kind of at a crossroad. You said you know my son is in the navy seals and he was having the same issue and program that helped and I'm in a leadership development program, so he said, I'll recommend you go to the same place and I know the lady there, I'll give her a call.

That's great. I said where is the locational head? So he told me and I said, you know what, I might do that. So we, we parted ways and left. So I said to myself, it's been so long since I took an order from anybody in the navy, instead of calling, I'm going to go right over there. So I went over there, took the costs, which was amazing and changed my life. And it was interesting probably; so about 10 years later I was at a cleaners and I heard a gentleman say, hey man, nice boots. And I turned around, I saw a cowboy boot dressed guy; he turned around and said, Paige. How is it going and how's your family? I said we're still going strong than ever and I've got a great relationship with my wife and children. I said how's it going with your son, a lieutenant in the navy seals? He Said, oh, my son is the youngest admiral in the navy, he hadn't been captured. It was kind of an interesting thing as I had hired that captain to come work for me. I started off scrubbing the shifts; some 20 years later I have the father of the son of the youngest admiral in the navy working for me.

Can you describe what drives you and your passion to do what you do and to help others?

Jimi Page: Funny some of the organizations that I sit on the board with; a salvation army, my local all county civic association, the alexander, a symphony orchestra; The Anacostia, a civic association or community center. Another thing is the DC chamber of commerce I belonged to. The reason why I got involved into the civic association is I found out that in life, one of the things that would never have been successful in my business if it wasn't for my relationship inside the community. In terms of poverty I guess the communities where they're at a disadvantage educationally, financially are the inner city.

Can you share an example of a project that you were able to work on and it became successful?

Jimi Page: When I first started my business, I couldn't afford the individuals that had a master's degree, doctor's degree, a business degree, you know, I was able to hire people that had certifications even though I found in some cases they were less reliable, but I've found that in some cases they will also leave and they will always be able to get me to a certain place and I'll never forget. There is a story about Babson College where my dad was a professor and it was interesting to him because most individuals at Baptist College wanted to own a business. Well he found it kind of senseless that only 10 percent of individuals that went to Babson College actually wanted to start their own business.

And he thought it just didn't make sense at all. So he did a one year study studying. What he did is he followed the top class people that top 10 percent because he wanted to find out the reason why individuals were not interested in starting a business and what was the reason why they did. So he followed the people and then he found out that, the ones who didn't start a business didn't start it because it was, they didn't have the education with the reason that; there was death in the family or that someone was having a baby or somebody who's married or there was a tragic event in the family or it was raining or snowing or the economy and the excuses go forth. When he found out that the 10 percent of people that actually started the business just started.

So he says, pretend you are standing at a door and there is a long corridor, imagine yourself taking a step inside the car and all of a sudden a door to the right or to the left opens so you have another choice and then you take another step and another door opens. So he said from the front door, you never see all of these doors that are available to you. The only way you see these doors is by actually stepping through them. Either the principal and I used that in my decisions, in what I do and the reason why I go down some of these of organs joining organizations and doing community work because it seems like another door opens and new chapter in my life with different people and find out how that relates to this journey that we're on.

What would you say to a valid fellow veteran who is seeking to go into business for themselves?

Jimi Page: I always use the analogy and I have got a picture of this on my wall of a mountain and a lot of people looking at success as climbing the mountain. Well, years ago people would climb a mountain and they get to the top of it and they say, wow,

I can see this and they get a better view of things that's coming up and let's say finally I made it to the top and then shortly after that, people started climbing a mountain and you know, instead of saying at that point, wow there you are, there you are and congratulating each other, I could see that children today, and a lot of millennial are climbing this mountain and they are taking selfies or they want to videotape themselves climbing a mountain to the top and say well all here I am, but I'm seeing a change in climbing this mountain and the picture that I have is; the top of the mountain is covered in clouds. And I'm finding out that there is no top to the mountain to climb but it is a journey. It's the people that you're climbing with, people that you help along the way to climb a mountain. But to think that there's a top of the mountain; to me, there's no top, it's clouded, it's covered, and the adventure, the joy and the satisfaction comes from the client.

What sets you apart from your competitors?

Jimi Page: What sets me apart from others is that I have an Uber mentality; so instead of having our clients come to us; we go to our clients. So I am the opposite of what normally happens like the Maytag repair where you call in for service and we go after. What we try to do is go out to clients and develop applications and service points that we can provide for them even before they ask for it.

About Jimi Page

Company:

Page Global

Who can I help: We help provide businesses with strong and durable office equipment; we equally manage documents and provide cyber security.

What sets me apart: We go to our customers to provide the services they need rather than stress them up to come look for us.

How to get in touch with us:

- Email: jimi.page@pageglobal.com
- Website: www.pageglobal.com

All You Need Is the Drive to Achieve Success! (Educator, Philosophy, Mentorship, Consulting, Speaking)

Discussion with Abdul Baytops

By providing consulting services to the federal government and private sector One Federal Solution (OFS) has effectively managed to turn a dream into reality from what started out as a man with a small vision of working with his friends. Abdul Baytops a U.S. Air force veteran is also the President and CEO of OFS, a company he has successfully ran for the last 14 years that focuses on providing IT technical services with a specialization in Emerging Technology. He nurtured and transformed a concept, which many would have taken for granted, into a suitable business success. Unlike many veterans and other new entrepreneurs, Abdul took advantage of the available resources at his disposal wheter big or small he recognized the advantage each could play in his long term dream. By virtues of his yearning passions and he was able to blend his military experience, discipline, accountability, and other values with his entrepreneurship skills to venture into the road to becoming a business owner. Abdul Baytops believes that understanding what you do and why you do it is the antidote in establishing meaningful creations.

Are you a veteran looking for ways to achieve success but maybe missing some key points to bridge the gap between failure and success? Abdul Baytops, like other entrepreneurs, was faced with many challenges but never took his eyes off the ultimate goal. He has enough experience from his military services and executive time leading OFS to help potential entrepreneurs expound on their endeavors. He believes that any entrepreneur can start from wherever they are and by using drive to can achieve favorable results. Read the story of his success and be inspired to cultivate your own prosperity.

Thank you so much for joining us today. Amongst many other areas of specialties, you are considered an expert in your field. Tell us your full name, professional title, and about your company.

My name is Abdul Baytops and I am the president and CEO of One Federal Solution (OFS) a consulting company that provides software development, data analytics, and cybersecurity services for the federal government and commercial customers. OFS focuses on providing lead technologies through an agile development framework for mission-critical initiatives. For the last 14 years, I have led this company to secure over $250 million in government contracts.

Briefly describe the outcome that can be achieved by working with you.

Abdul Baytops: The outcome will vary based on the client and their specific need but I can say with certainty when you are working with me or my team we strive understand where you are at in order to see where you want to go before we try to implement of suggest a solution. By doing this we are able to provide you with results that have immediate impact on your business bottom line rather than heavy investments and limited results because the requirement was not correctly interpreted. I tell both our new and existing customers to give OFS a chance to challenge your way of thinking if you really want to see cart start to move.

Tell us why you think your business is important. What are the benefits of working with a company like yours?

Abdul Baytops: OFS was started to work with companies and use innovation to take them to then next level and stay ahead of their competitors by using metrics and data to manage your success. We work hard to find out what is it that the client wants and then offer them the proper solution that matches their ultimate business goals to meet their projected results in an agile environment. We also make sure that the people, the strategists that we hire, are experienced and successful as well so I clients always know through our experience we have provided them with the technical experts needed for the next level of success.

What stirred you to move in this professional direction?

Abdul Baytops: I started out in the United States Air Force. I was working as an aerospace technician at Andrews Air Force Base. It was a totally different career path, filled with totally different choices to make compared to where I am now. I was there, in the Air Force base, working with U.S. pilots and foreign executive dignitaries but at the same time I was reading about how to be a systems administrator and troubleshooting pc repairs in which later would spark my IT interest. Though I had this interest in a completely different career field I stayed in the Air Force and continued my tour of duty until I was honorably discharged. Later, I began working at a few nonprofits in the Washington, D.C., area, doing things like administrative functions, print shop, logo design, web design and minor pc repair work after hours. Eventually after many attempts I was then given the opportunity to work with a company to become finally someone on the IT team as an Application Engineer. This experience paved way for the rest of my career.

This opened up my imagination to what else exists in the world of technology and also lit the entrepreneur bug that secretly was hiding in head as well. I continued performing IT roles for about 4 years and became extremely curious about self employment, creating my own footprint, my own future, and controlling my own path. I felt like I would rather define my own future based on my preferred work habits and technical skills. Consequently, I started my company roughly 15 years later.

Typically, how long does it take to recoup an investment in this business?

Abdul Baytops: I cant say there is a correct answer to this due to the amount of variables that have to be considered in each business and the specifics that go along with the services being offered and also the management of the company itself but I can say without hesitation business is a risk and with any risk sometimes you win and other time you lose. On occasions some may lose more than other but that not necessarily is not a bad thing but allows for an internal look at the business plan and rapid adoption of new steps to lead to your success.

What resources have you used or had access to that you feel benefited you professionally to grow your business and is exclusive to veterans?

Abdul Baytops: I have used various resources over the last 15 years, so it is somehow hard to just say one in particular. As with any business, it takes a lot of things to come together to be successful. An SDVOSB veteran benefit I have participated in are veteran-owned small business conferences that focus on meeting and building relationships with other companies, vendors, and CEO's. I also routinely work to attend working groups in areas I believe are the next wave of growth in order to forge new relationships and also continually challenge myself.

Establishing a network of peers has also helped educate me on specific failures and successes as I journey down the road of business. Relationships are also very important along with diversity and need to come from all aspects of business along with maintaining a balance life with your inner self as well.

What misconceptions and fears have you had and have found that fellow veterans have about venturing into this line of entrepreneurship and how did you resolve it?

Abdul Baytops: One profound fear that I, and my fellow veterans, tend to have is the fear of the unknown. It is not uncommon for veterans to be put into a uncontrolled/confined space; I believe that the military structure and framework becomes a part of you. You really cannot fail if you realize what good and bad things you may have to face before you and know that failure is just a step away from achieving success.

What tools and education did you receive during your military service career that helped you reach your level of success in business today?

Abdul Baytops: The number one tool that I received from my time in the military was "Integrity" and "Organizational skills" in additional the ability to perform critical thinking.   The military also allowed me to attend several colleges during my enlistment to include the University of Central Florida, Valencia College, University of Maryland and Liberty University each one adding additional fuel that continuously fuels my way of thinking.

What do you think any veteran should know before deciding to venture into entrepreneurship?

Abdul Baytops: The key thing I think any veterans should know before they decide to venture into entrepreneurship is, it will be a tough, hard road, but you have to stay the course. The same thing you learned when you were in the military—just stay the course until the end. You will encounter many obstacles along the way, but just stay positive, stay focused. Be truthful to yourself. A lot of times people do not want to really admit that they are failing, and then they continue to fail some more and can never get out.

But the truth is, you have to identify your failure and be able to face your view. I am a person who thinks that once you do face your reality whether good or bad, you will be able to come back out to the top again. There are many books that I have read—people who tried one, two, three, four, five companies before they were finally successful. I heard that the CEO of Amazon tried hundreds of people before he was successful in getting his first investor, and now look at it ... So, you just have to stay to course; believe in yourself; and understand where you are, your idea, and your business.

How can you help a veteran who is interested in business achieve the greatest success?

Abdul Baytops: I believe that in order to achieve the greatest success you need to establish the proper mentor/mentee relationships. Mentoring could include teaching them how to succeed with no money, how to succeed in an certain environment where there are always too many of the same products or services. The basis of my teaching principles involves positivity, being positive about yourself as a veteran, and overall person. This is the reason why my company has been around for over 14 years.

However, I was not always this positive. Initially OFS was focused on health care professionals who worked at home. I was having a hard time orchestrating my time and on top of that losing revenue. This was my first encounter with failure, so I thought. This moment was a turning point. I learned valuable lesson, such as time management, and strategic planning. It's likely that if I stuck to that market, I would probably be back in the employee workforce. I enjoy helping people, and it is important to note that failing is only temporary. Everyone has infinite potential; however, sometimes it takes a little support."

Can you share a lesson you learned early in your career as a business leader that you overcame and now makes you the go-to person for your prospective clients?

Abdul Baytops: I would say a valuable lesson I learned early in my career is to be your true, authentic to yourself. My strategy is to let the customer know who are and that you can be trusted. When I am pursuing new clients, I keep that into perspective at all time because there are hundreds of companies that can offer the same services so I try to offer them that personal touch.

What's the most important question veterans should ask themselves as they consider where they are today, where they want to be tomorrow, and how they plan to get there?

Abdul Baytops: I think one of the most important questions a veteran should ask is, "Where do you see yourself tomorrow?" Like me, you may spent a lot of time in the military, and time is something that you can never get back. So, the question is, "How much time do I have left on the clock until my ideas and thought process is no longer relevant? What is it that I am trying to do and how can I get there?" It goes back to what I said earlier, which is, having a plan. What is your plan to get there? Is it realistic? Is it attainable? You have to be honest with yourself, and if you are able to answer these questions authentically, then you have a realistic plan, and you will exceed the expectations that you set forth for yourself.

But you just have to be honest and open with yourself. You need to know where are you *today* and where you want to go *tomorrow*. I am very focused, always planned, and driven. I know many people who started companies without a plan, and six months down the road, they were overwhelmed thinking, "Man, we are not making money. What was the plan when we started? We figured we would start marketing five months after we started working, but we did not realize we were going to run out of money." Again, having a concrete plan is the catalyst in realizing your ultimate goals.

What three qualities should a veteran reading your chapter consider when choosing to venture into business?

Abdul Baytops:

1. You need to know your intended market and be committed to it; you must be able to plan effectively; you should perform regular self-evaluation. Business is what you make it. My business has been the best thing I have ever done though at times I had some years that were good and at times some that were bad "Life is what you make it". As long as you stay on course, you can be very successful with it because, like every plan and every path, you have to learn that eventually, everything will fall in place.
2. Veterans considering business should be prepared for the ups and downs. If you cannot handle rough patches that life may throw at you being a business owner may not be for you.
3. Lastly self-evaluations of where you are in life and business. You must be willing to evaluate yourself to know where you are as you journey down this road. Sometimes as you are hiking down the paths of life it may require some course corrections so this is important as you take these steps.

What sets you and your company apart from your competitors?

Abdul Baytops: What sets us apart from our competitors is, our team dynamic. OFS is equipped with a team of technical experts each working to change how innovation can work for our customers. Myself being a veteran, I bring the experience I gained while working with the Federal Government and other companies in terms my experience in data analytics, strategic coaching, mentoring, and financial management as well as goal setting. In additional my partners bring government experience, an abundance of software development skills, data analytics, data science, and so much more. Ultimately, OFS is destined to be a successful team.

About Abdul Baytops

Company:

One Federal Solution

Who can I help? I aim to help you find success in whatever your dream is and work with you to unlock the possibilities within it.

What sets me apart: I believe the journey I have taken to get to where I am can assist others with roadblocks they may encounter along the way. While many people have failed along the road to be an entrepreneur including me I take those building blocks and assist you in creating a better future.

How to get in touch with us:

§ Email: abaytops@onefederalsolution.com

§ Website: onefederalsolution.com and successtheonlyoption.com

§ Social media: successtheonlyoption

CHAPTER NINE

Negotiate with Confidence
Discussion with William Belknap

William Belknap, a US Army veteran, learned confidence, leadership skills, team building and professional skill sets from the military. He combined these incredible values and attributes to start his facility Maintenance, Repair and Operations (MRO) company which, provides maintenance and repair and, operational services to the federal and state governments. His value proposition and focus is to provide traditional mechanical, electrical and plumbing, minor renovations and other facility services for Veteran Affairs Medical Centers, and the National Cemetery Administration. He and his wife's company support a nonprofit that grants needs and "bucket list" wishes to deserving seniors. It is called Twilight Wish Foundation. One third of the wishes are granted to veterans. His company has a culture of completing every project on time, within budget, to a high degree of quality and, with zero safety incidents. To achieve this goal, he hires site superintendents and various trades such as mechanical technicians, electricians, carpenters, and others to complete projects on schedule.

William's experience came from courses he took in the military, preparing him for individual assignments. Some of these courses include, contract and price negotiation, other federal government acquisition courses, logistics training, and construction and vendor management. He also attended numerous government procurement conferences to build relationships and understand his client's future requirements and problem sets. He also networked with fellow veterans from the Army, Navy, and Air Force to learn and grow partnerships. These partnerships would become mutually beneficial business relationships that the government would hire to perform MRO services at their facilities.

As a prospecting entrepreneur, the real challenges to face are managing and balancing your business, developing your business plan, vetting it with experts at numerous organizations, and the launching of your company. Should you choose to tread William's line of business, government contracting and managing of facilities are two great strengths that demand absolute commitment and hard work. His zeal for entrepreneurship came from decades of subscribing to numerous business publications such as Forbes, Fortune, Inc and Entrepreneur magazines. He also learned from a Small Business Administration report that veterans businesses are key components of economic growth for the US economy. Thus, the federal government has a great need and desire to constantly foster the start-up and growth of new businesses. William wants veterans to do business with a living, breathing, and constantly changing dynamism that requires them to know and keep their audience as clients. According to him, "If others can do business and succeed, so can veterans. Strive to focus on your true strength; create a value proposition for potential customers and have passion for your company."

Enjoy reading from this great treasure of success!

Introduction

As a child in the 1960's, I purchased a book for 99 cents, "1001 Things You Can Get for Free." I had an insatiable appetite for learning and experiencing things. I grew up on a farm in Indiana where the nearest neighbor was a quarter mile down the road. I had a very "modest" income from picking up discarded coke bottles on the side of the road for 5 cents and recycling them. And, a I had a passion to receive mail: it was one of my connections to the world beyond my farm. I thought the book was a perfect fit. Yes, this was before the internet. I would write to the American Heart Association and ask for their free booklet on a healthy heart. I would write to countries at the United Nations and ask for information about their country. I would write to major league baseball teams and ask for a free sticker, baseball player or team picture. I always thought from an early age, what a Great Nation we live in that is so full of opportunities.

In school, I would participate in numerous "free" activities to experience them and make contributions where I could. These activities included, an eighth-grade science fair, in High School the following – Speech Team, Drama Club, Basketball Team, Wrestling Team, Baseball Team, Travelling Swing Choir etc. etc. etc. These experiences provided a forum for me to determine what I enjoyed, was good at and, did not enjoy. I received my bachelor's degree for free – West Point. I travelled on jets overseas for free – Space A, to over a dozen countries. I obtained my master's degree nearly for free. You get the picture. In the United States of America, we live in a land of incredible promise, opportunity and experiences unmatched any where in the world.

Starting a company there are numerous free or mostly free services available to help start and grow small businesses in the United States. For a "Tip of the Iceberg" list, there's the Small Business Administration (SBA), Small Business Development Center (SBDC), Veterans Business Outreach Centers (VBOC), Veterans Institute for Procurement (VIP) etc. etc. All of these services can either provide direct advice or, refer to another service provider who can answer almost any aspect of starting and running a small business. These are all opportunities for success!

Two other extremely important extremely important considerations for starting your business are, knowing the competitive products or services you bring to clients and, what are you passionate about doing. Many veterans today will become successful in entrepreneurship when they discover and apply this strategy. I started my company from scratch with my wife as my partner. She combines her accounting expertise with fiery marketing skills to handle invoicing, taxes, and financial reporting. I, on the other hand, handle business development, networking, and project management in starting my facility maintenance, repair and operation's (MRO) services company

Thank you so much for joining us today. Amongst many other areas of specialty, you are considered an expert in your field. Please tell us your full name, your professional title, and about your company.

William Belknap: My name is William Belknap. I'm the president and CEO of AEONRG LLC. We provide maintenance, repair, and other facility services to federal and state governments. We are now focusing almost exclusively on the Veteran Affairs Medical Centers and the National Cemetery Administration. Traditional services AEONRG LLC performs are mechanical, electrical, plumbing as well as ground maintenance. We have been in business for seven years and have been awarded over 150 government contracts, geographically ranging from Buffalo, New York, down to Asheville, North Carolina. We have employed approximately 50 individuals, mostly part-time, for various contracts that we have been awarded; many of them are veterans from the various services, Army, Air Force, Navy, Marines, and Coast Guard. We take great pride in providing all of our services and projects with three main characteristics. Number one, projects are completed on time; number two, they are accomplished to a high degree of quality; and number three, they are performed with zero safety incidences. To date, all 150 projects, have been successful in achieving our top three attributes. We partner with numerous individuals, technicians, and experts in their fields, and we take great pride in our partnerships. We treat our partners they way we would want to be treated as a valuable contributing team member. We also take great pride in knowing that the services we provide the VA medical centers and also the national cemetery administration directly impact the quality of life of veterans and their families.

Mention one big problem you specialize in solving.

William Belknap: One of the big problems or I would say challenges that we face is that not all government solicitations are as specific as they need to be to perform the task or project that needs to be accomplished. And with those projects, I always say that it's important once you're awarded a government contract to sit down with the customer to fully understand their expectations. Ensure the problem or tasks at hand are well defined and agreed by both parties – customer and contractor. And even though you have provided your proposal, even though the government provided drawings and specifications in the solicitation, it's extremely important to meet with the customer for a kickoff meeting and again, set expectations. Setting expectations on outcomes is absolutely critical for the success of a project. The best communication by far is face to face where you can look at them in the eye and see their facial expressions and the way they communicate. This also begins to immediately build trust.

Our number one priority for every single project we do is safety. Safety, in that no one gets hurt. Safety in that we do no harm to the operations of the client; we emphasize training, briefings and the buddy system to reduce risk. We have an extensive safety policy; we have a safety implementation task sheet. Safety has to be earned.

The other outcome is our timing - when do we expect to do certain parts of a project. This timing directly affects the positive quality project outcomes. Setting those expectations with the customer, meeting them face to face is absolutely critical toward a successful project. So, besides setting expectations, another problem we face is further understanding what the government wants from some of the solicitations they post. And with that method, it's important to reach out to the contract specialist or the contracting officers within the government, ask Q&A's or call them for a formal dialogue. Conducting these are one of my strengths.

Tell us why you think your business is important. What are the benefits of working with a company like yours?

William Belknap: My business is competitive and passionate in what we do for a couple of reasons. We provide mechanical, electrical, plumbing, and other facility services to ensure that the veterans affairs' medical centers are running in a highly proficient manner, as it all boils down to providing world-class care to our veterans' health. Those that are serving, those that are in the reserves, those that are potentially part-time, and those that have served our country, we want to make sure that they have the highest quality mechanical, electrical, plumbing, and other facility services as possible that the VA can provide. The services we specialize in are maintenance repair and minor construction. I note that specifically because it aligns well with my past experience, past performance and high proficiency for managing facilities.

Another benefit of working with a company like AEONRG is that we provide experienced problem-solving and high customer relationship development. This leads to the efficient execution of projects and services in a cost-effective, timely manner that, is conducted on schedule to a high degree of quality and, with zero safety incidences. Customers like us because, they know they can trust us. They trust us because of past performance and because of delivering on our numerous commitments.

I want my customers to know that one of my goals with running the company is reputation, and knowing that I'm doing something for a higher cause—helping veterans' health, helping those that have fought for our country, helping those that are served our nation, which of course is an all-volunteer force. Less than 1% of the nation now has served our country. And it's important, in my view, to take care of those that have volunteered and put themselves potentially in harm's way and, take care of them as the government promised they would. We are also straightforward; thus, our clients are not going to experience drama with our company because we are a company that is focused on getting the project done in the right manner.

Another benefit of working with AEONRG LLC is that as a small company, we are very nimble, so we can quickly adapt to changing circumstances. We aren't afraid to recommend positive contract changes to the government that might lower costs or, provide a higher quality product or, increase services for our veterans. One example occurred when AEONRG was hired to address a sinkhole at the VA Medical Center in Lebanon, Pennsylvania. The bottom of the sinkhole to be addressed and fixed wasn't visible from the surface of the ground. So, there was uncertainty as to what was below the sinkhole and, the root cause of its development. We brought in geotechnical engineers who had handled these types of problems before, especially in the medical center's limestone environment.

I'm proud to state that once we started digging into the sinkhole, we found the root cause of the problem. We recommend to the government a modification to the contract that reduced the government's project cost. The contract had required the removal and return of a 3000-gallon underground water tank. After testing the integrity of the tank, we recommended to the government that we take that out of our scope (remove and return) since there was no need to do that. That caused us to get a change order and reduce the cost of the government substantially. With the money saved, the government was able to do other safety initiatives for the medical center, which included installing bollards around fire hydrant and extending sidewalks.

What stirred you to move in this professional direction? Include a short story about how you caught the bug to do what you do? Describe what drives you and your passion to do what you do and to help others.

William Belknap: I received training and experience of managing a facility during one of my earlier assignments in the military. In the military, especially within the officer career track, you have a combat arms specialty and a functional area. My combat arms specialty was armor which, I spent a decade with command and staff positions with armor troops. My first assignment was as a M60A3 Tank Platoon leader where my General Defensive Plan position was near the Fulda Gap, near the East-West German border in the early 1980's. After several battalion and brigade staff positions, I then commanded an Abrams tank company at Fort Stewart, Georgia. After I finished those ten years of command and staff assignments, I was then assigned to my functional area, other positions that must be filled by Army Officers. At one point in time, I was made the construction contracting officer for an army base. The military base was north of Detroit. I became a contracting officer after receiving schooling and training, which was quite extensive; actually, it was about 10 different courses and fellowships. I had to gain work experience, and I had to achieve results.

After my contracting officer assignment, I was appointed as the Deputy Army Installation Commander. My responsibilities and oversight were the installation's engineers, logisticians, human resources and financial services. On the military base, we had units from all branches of the Services. And, we were also located next to Michigan Air National Guard units. I managed the installation's facility maintenance and repair and operation's services. I enjoyed the challenges and taking care of military servicemen and women and their families. The satisfaction of taking care of veterans' families here drove me or helped me to find my first job after my military career which, was to run a corporate facility for about a decade with Pfizer, Inc where, I did many similar tasks. I managed subcontractors to keep the facility up and running. I constantly studies and incorporated best practices and into the facility's MRO services.

While stationed as a Deputy Army Installation Commander, I received other unexpected tasks such as working with the secret service when the presidential candidates flew into the military base in 1992, President Bush at the time and, future President Clinton. We were charged with working with them, bringing families to the tarmac to greet the presidential candidates while they were campaigning. We were charged with executing numerous other community events, facilitating an air show that happened on the runways of the facility, as well as taking care of many visitors that would come to the site.

So, those are some of the things I experienced. I have always had passion to add more value to any position I'm assigned. This included my Pfizer corporate location. One of the accomplishments I'm most proud of is bringing in a new training methodology for the division of Pfizer I supported, Pfizer Animal Health. This was a $4 billion division of the $50 billion company. I founded the learning center for this division of the company. Since the Animal Health division had 650 field sales force representatives, I thought they would benefit from more realistic training, like the realistic training I received in the military to become proficient in my job. Since the sales reps sold drug and medications to veterinary clinics, it seemed to me the reps should train in a mock vet clinic at my facility. Thus, I founded the Pfizer Animal Health Learning Center. Before the Center field sales force reps trained in several Marriott and Hilton properties across the country – not realistic training.

Typically, how long does it take to recoup an investment in your business?

William Belknap: Personally and financially, the ROI was about 5 years. Then, the upside significantly increased. For the services we perform, the return on investment for what we do is immediate for our customers. For example, once we provide a chiller replacement for a medical center, the Center was immediately able to use the new chiller for its patients. In this case, we're doing one for an operating room, and once we have it installed, they'll have immediate access to the cooling for their various rooms. As far as return on investment, I suppose, for the federal government, it's a different value proposition. The federal government typically receives its annual budget, and from that annual budget, they look to their capital asset managers to acquire the funds needed to fund those capital projects. So, the government doesn't necessarily look for a profit or return on investment like a corporation might. However, it does have a planned budget, and this forms the list of things that have to be replaced, repaired, or fixed. So, our value proposition is that we complete projects on time.

What resource have you used or had access to that you feel benefited you professionally to grow your business and is exclusive to veterans?

William Belknap: Resources that are available to veteran entrepreneurs are numerous; much of them are free, and some are low cost. And those that are willing to pay can pay an unlimited amount for consulting resources. Let's start with what's available free of charge to veterans, small businesses. The Small Business Administration (SBA) helps individuals to start their own businesses and, that includes veterans. Typically, veterans will be hired within the SBA as mentors for other veterans. I would highly recommend going to the SBA regional office, introduce yourself to an advisor, inform them where you ae in the development of yourbusiness, and begin a professional relationship. For me, there's a Small Business Administration office located in the city of King of Prussia that, serves the Philadelphia Region. I have taken several courses and seminars with them. I have attended a federal government contracting course and a course on how to do business with the government. For me, it was a reemergence back into federal government contracting, understanding the latest, regulations and, becoming efficient again in maneuvering through them.

The second part of the SBA would be having a mentor whom you can ask specific questions and get clarification on various rules and regulations to make sure you're compliant. At the SBA Office you can also discuss challenges or seek advice, such as vetting your business plan or obtaining guidance on implementing your business plan. Or, if you have questions about the federal government contracts in general, there's an opportunity to ask them and receive answers from experts. Another resource is the Small Business Development Center (SBDC). They help to provide advice about securing government contracts, through financial support from the Defense Logistics Agency. They also provide solicitation leads and opportunities and, send them directly to your email inbox once a day if you sign up for that free service. Conduct a "google" search for the nearest one in your area.

The Veterans Business Outreach Center (VBOC) is a specific center for veterans to get advice on various business ownership questions. Another veteran-specific opportunity is the VIP that is sponsored by the Montgomery County Chamber outside of Washington D.C. VIP stands for Veterans Institute of Procurement. A scholarship is offered to attend for those that apply and are chosen. This is a week of intensive training on federal government procurement and best business practices.

To gain potential financial resources and clarity and vetting of your business value proposition, there are also several veteran shark tank events. As example, the Greater Philadelphia Veterans Network's (GPVN) Shark Tank is now National with sub competitions in San Antonio, Detroit and Seattle. The winners will all meet in Philadelphia at the end of 2019. During the 2018 Shark Tank, the winning veteran company was awarded a $25,000 grant to continue and expand their business. This year they'll win a $50,000 grant. So, as you can see, it is quite an amazing opportunity for veterans to be awarded financial resources to be able to launch their company, grow it even farther and, improve their business plan. Success in the commercial or government sectors is all about developing relationships, learning from your peers, partnering with your peers to start and grow your company.

Another of my favorite veteran procurement organization is the National Veterans Small Business Council (NVSBC). It provides grants to deserving veterans to attend their annual procurement conference. Recently, I was honored to facilitate another veteran receiving a full grant, meaning their lodging, as well as transportation to this three-day procurement conference, is paid for. There, there are numerous opportunities for seminars, networking and meeting potential customers.

What misconceptions and fears have you found that fellow veterans may have about venturing into a line of entrepreneurship and how did you resolve it?

William Belknap: One of the fears that veterans have about starting a business is: "How do I support myself while starting the business?" If you have a job, there's a perception that you have security with your job and a constant paycheck. Conversely, there's the perception that there are significant risks and unknowns about starting a business. The reality is that as a small business owner, the only one that can "fire" you is, yourself. Working for a company you are typically working for that company and can be let go at any time. Thus, in many cases, being your own boss has greater job security. As for how can start a business, my philosophy has been; If other individuals can do it, I can do it." If other individuals can start a company successfully and flourish, I can do it.

Financial means to start your company or, support yourself until the new company is self-supporting can include: 1. Maintaining a full or part time job; 2. Save money from a previous job; 3. Obtain money from friends and family; 4. Obtain crowd sourcing; 5. Obtain a loan or, 6. Find other sources of funding from various investor groups such as Angel Investors. Both the SBA, the Service Corps of Retired Executives or simply, SCORE can provide mentors for advice and guidance on how to proceed with your company. SCORE can offer you a Board of Advisors. Their website is packed with numerous resources for starting and growing small businesses. I personally have used a combination of resources, savings, an inheritance, and a severance package from a corporation to financially support my family while starting my company.

What tools and education did you receive during your military service career that helped you reach your level of success in business today?

William Belknap: Many of the tools I received in the military to obtain the level of success in business I have achieved today were from the training I received during a 20-year military career and 10-year corporate career. In the military, I found that with each new assignment, there's always preparation for each job you are assigned. Many of these skills are directly applicable to running a company.

For example, in my military career, I learned about managing vendors or subcontractors while assigned in a leadership role running a military installation. I was also trained at Pfizer. I learned the skill sets to become a contracting officer (CO) in the Army. To be a qualified CO, there are about 10 different schools and experiences that are required. A follow-on experience was being assigned as a contract specialist putting together proposals, solicitations for maintenance and repair solicitations. I was also a contracting officer for a facility. This position gave me expertise in federal government contracting. And, there are many other skill sets and certification opportunities such as program management, that you receive in the military that are applicable to a commercial industry and running a business.

What do you think any veterans should know before deciding to venture into entrepreneurship?

William Belknap: There are primarily two things that you should know before starting your professional career of becoming an entrepreneur. Number one is, what are your skill sets? What are the values that you bring to the table that customers would want to pay for?

Number two, what is your passion? What turns you on to go to work every day? What is it of value that you bring to the table that people, government or business value and would pay for? What is it that excites you to get up in the morning, and makes you want to go to work and provide your customers competitive products and/or services? What goals do you want to achieve? So, those are the primary things I would say you'd have to decide on before you become an entrepreneur.

With the knowledge of these, you develop a business plan from readily available software programs, free templates from organizations such as SCORE or the SBA. Your business plan could be long-term or short-term but, I absolutely believe that you need to have some sort of a business plan put down in writing. Answer questions on the business plans addressing the word "How." How are you going to achieve your goals? How will you obtain the resources you need. How are you going to obtain resources? How are you going market your products or services? How will you obtain financing or the certifications you may need? These are some of the considerations before you venture into entrepreneurship.

How you can help a veteran who is interested in business achieve the greatest success?

William Belknap: Helping veterans achieve success is one of my passions, and I do that by giving back. I have helped numerous veterans, just as many veterans and successful business executive have helped me to be a successful business owner. My assistance to others emanates from achieving success in federal government contracting, running a military installation and, operating a facility as a site general manager, a facility manager within a large corporation. Since I cannot always directly help those who helped me, I pass it down. I would challenge any veteran that once you have become successful, that in some way, shape or form you pass down your success to other so that we all continue this legacy of veterans helping veterans succeed.

I also participate in numerous military organizations where I meet other veterans, and I facilitate helping them to start companies. This participation is an opportunity to give back, pass what I've received and learned, down to the next group of veterans.

I've also helped facilitate the growth of the Greater Philadelphia Veterans' Network Shark Tank, which is now national, and as Board of Directors member of the Chester County Chamber of Business and Industry I have given advice to numerous small business owners. . This year, I was elected a Board of Trustees' member for the National Small Business Association. Indirectly, I am helping to shape a policy within our country, within specific legislation, to make sure that small businesses remain competitive against large businesses, be it tax reforms, affordable health care or regulations reduction. All of these are ways that I give back.

Can you share an example of a project that you were able to work on, and it became successful?

William Belknap: An example of a project where I was successful was one of the earlier government contracts that I was awarded, which was to retube a industrial sized boiler at a medical center. Simplistically, a boiler is the shape of a very large "coke can." And, inside the coke can is a bunch of tubes such as there are in a car radiator. The tubes are filled with water and the large flame inside heats up the water that goes through the tubes. This steam then is moved throughout the medical center to provide heat. The tubes need to be retubed, meaning taking out the old tubes and putting new tubes about once every 30 years. It was a project that I wanted to pursue, and I needed to find a technical partner and technicians who had extensive experience in successfully performing these types of projects. I got a referral to find someone through a company that I wanted to work with, and this then led to a wonderful partnership where I managed the project, including the administration and customer interface. The technicians performing the work were able to retube that boiler successfully within the cost and schedule I provided. So, that's an example of a successful project I worked on despite the challenges; finding the technical expertise that I did not particularly have in-house to essentially complete a project.

Can you share a lesson you learned early in your career as a business leader that you overcame and now makes you the go-to person for your prospective clients?

William Belknap: I would say the challenges I overcame include more fully understanding, responding to government solicitations and doing it in an efficient manner and in a manner that robustly answers the questions, provides the information the government seeks to ascertain that you're technically acceptable and highly qualified to perform a project. My staff and I ensure that our proposals are compliant and legal. A competitive advantage I offer customers is that my company is available when the government needs something done quickly. We have developed long-term relationships and a reputation that AEONRG will provide quality services on time and zero safety incidences. With that reputation and experience, the government is willing to allow us to bid on projects and win them because they know that their projects will be accomplished in a quality, efficient manner.

What's the most important question veterans should ask themselves as they consider where they are today, where they want to be tomorrow, and how they plan to get there?

William Belknap: You need to have a plan. It's better to have a plan than not have a plan. A plan means setting long range goals – three to five years in the future and then, intermediate steps to reach those long-term goals. As an entrepreneur, you also need flexibility. You need flexibility to adapt to changing competitive realities your business must address. You can always adjust your plan. However, it's absolutely necessary to have a plan to guide your day to day actions that will lead toward achieving long term outcomes. Otherwise, there is substantial risk constantly changing your tasks at hand and, actually not getting anything done!

As a veteran entrepreneur starting a company, you need to have a timeframe of when you are going to have your business plan done as well as when and how you're going to obtain financing. In your business plan you will be addressing numerous questions such as "How are you going to get financing to pay new hires?" "What do you want to be doing tomorrow, and how do you get there?" Also address, "How do I obtain help to answer questions or assist in solving problems."

What three qualities should a veteran reading your chapter consider when choosing to venture into business?

William Belknap: Number one is a sense of attitude that if others can do it, I can do it. Number two, is being fearless and confident in a manner that you'll be able to achieve and be successful. Number three, I would suggest a quality to possess is the no-quit military spirit, like when in combat where there is no option; you do not quit! You were trained to do your job in the most challenging of circumstances. These circumstance might have been being under enemy fire, experiencing extreme heat or cold, lacking food or water, etc. You overcame these challenges. You didn't quit. You never quit.

What sets you and your company apart from your competitors?

William Belknap: What sets AEONRG apart from other companies is that My Team and I have the ability to adapt to changing environments or conditions. We are able to provide best value services for the customer and, over communicate with customers to ensure expectations are met and hopefully exceeded. Another competitive attribute is that AEONRG LLC provides services in a cost-effective manner to our government clients. The government has a set price tag for overhead and profitability, and some may want to exceed that. However, given that the government is allocating taxpayer's money, I have a significant understanding of where we need to be price-wise. We have a significant understanding of what we need to do to be competitive while providing the quality services that we provide and, demonstrate that to our government clients. Also important is our reputation, experience, and ability to demonstrate exceptional performance in a high-quality manner. We ensure that we have an exemplary safety record while we work with a government client to compete a project on time with a high degree of quality.

About William Belknap

Company:

AEONRG, LLC

Who can I help: We provide maintenance, repair, and other facility services (MRO) to the federal government, specifically to the Veterans Affairs.

What sets me apart: We always make sure to carry out all our projects in a timely manner, and the safety of our clients is our utmost priority.

How to get in touch with us:

- Email: bill.belknap@aeonrg.com
- Website: www.aeonrg.com

CHAPTER TEN

Developing Courage to Sell 'You'

Discussion with Bill Irwin

Many family-owned businesses don't exist beyond the life span of their founders or into another generation—but not with Bill Irwin! Bill Irwin, a U.S. Marine Corps veteran understands the importance of business communication with innovative technology to inherit and moved Data-Line Office Systems, a family-owned business, to the next level and provide clients with solutions. Fully armed with utmost entrepreneurship skills to develop courage and sell his ideas, Bill Irwin used his B2B (business to business) company to sell and service office equipment such as copiers, scanners, fax machines, shredders, and folding machines to his clients. He carved a niche for himself in Data-Line Office Systems with a dedicated team of trained technicians who are ready to meet the slightest needs of their clients within the timeline of demand. Nothing can be better than a sound customer support that a business can offer at the right time to keep clients' businesses running unhindered. That was the much Bill Irwin was up to in meeting the office and site needs of his clients.

Bill Irwin offers a central billing system to ensure that there is a satisfactory delivery of services to his clients. To avoid the challenges of multiple vendors, Bill Irwin will personally handle all the paper works in shipping and the returning of the equipment to allow him optimize every sales opportunity within the country. He appointed an authorized dealer to ship the purchased equipment to wherever they are needed. The dealers are contacted at the slightest time of their sales needs, and in return, they will hand Data-Line Office Systems their shipping bills, which is incorporated into the client's overall payment, with ease.

To succeed in business either as a veteran or would-be entrepreneur, endeavor to give your clients absolute listening ears. Like Bill Irwin, you can grow your business annually by 15% with developed courage to sell what you do as an entrepreneur. Most people, especially veterans, don't understand the importance of financial discipline, good listening technique, quality leadership, reliability, confidence, and understanding that are required to keep their clients in the modern-day industry. The story of Data-Line Office Systems can help you to connect with Bill Irwin to work smart, manage your clients, and develop courage to sell yourself with huge profits.

Thank you so much for joining us today. Amongst many other areas of specialty, you are considered an expert in your field. Tell us your full name, professional title, and about your company.

My name is Bill Guy Irwin. I am the President and full owner of Data-Line Office Systems in Lubbock, Texas. My company was formed over 37 years ago by my father and a good friend and colleague. They were the best in town in the sales and repair of copiers. They felt underappreciated where they were, so they formed the new company. I started as warehouse man and deliveryman. Over the years, I have held every position in the company, except bookkeeper. I bought the business from my father in 2006.

Tell us why you think your business is important? What are the benefits of working with a company like yours?

Like it or not, we still live in a world that creates a lot of paper documents. We use less printer paper every year, but it will take decades for us to ever get near a 'paperless society.' Have you signed a mortgage lately? No one in the world is an expert at everything. It would be absurd for a doctor, lawyer, or accountant to try disassembling today's high-tech devices, trying to figure out why it won't work. Working with a locally owned business creates a feeling of family, both with the employees and with the clientele. Someone with a local accent answers the phone.

What stirred you to move in this professional direction?

In college, I dreamed of becoming an engineer, but while I was going to school, I was also working for my father. Every day, I saw happy faces in our customers' offices because we were solving problems for them. Additionally, our employees loved and respected my father. I came to understand that no matter what profession I entered, if I did it well, I would make a difference in other people's lives. So, I took the path of least resistance and went to work full-time.

Describe what drives you and your passion to do what you do and help the people you help.

I'm driven because I know that I'm needed. Almost everybody copies, prints, scans, or folds something. With 37 years of experience, I can help someone with good advice and explain how I came to that conclusion. It is very satisfying when, later, they thank me or refer me to their associates.

Typically, how long does it take to recoup an investment in this business?

To start from scratch, I believe that it would take three hard years to recover expenses in a start up in this industry.

What resource have you used or had access to that you feel benefited you professionally to grow your business and is exclusive to veterans?

Giving up is not an option. I didn't try this planning to lose. Create a smart strategy and then execute it.

What tools and education did you receive during your military service career that helped you to reach your level of success in business today?

I received a great work ethic, understanding that if you must work long hours and weekends to succeed, then that is what you do. Respect everyone, unless they give you a reason not to respect them. Always dress for success.

What do you think any veteran should know before they decide to venture into entrepreneurship?

Make sure that you are prepared with the knowledge and skills for the industry you plan to enter. Study your future competition. Make sure you have money to lose for the first year.

How can you help a veteran who is interested in business achieve the greatest success?

Understand that ninety percent of your time in the beginning should be spent networking with other professionals. Join the Chamber of Commerce; go to all the events. The more hands you shake, the more money you will make.

Can you share an example of a project that you were able to work on, and it became successful?

I won a bid at a school district for equipment and maintenance. I did my homework and figured out that they weren't going to need anywhere near the amount of maintenance that they requested in the bid. I calculated a more reasonable number and based my quote on that figure. I agreed to what they were asking for, knowing that I would only be fulfilling their needs with less than half the work that they were requesting.

Can you share a lesson you learned early in your career as a business leader that you overcame and now makes you the go-to person for your prospective clients?

Sell the customer what they want to buy. Offer an alternative that your experience has taught you would be a better choice. But don't try to force your recommendation on the customer. Once again, sell the customer what they want to buy.

What's the most important question veterans should ask themselves as they consider where they are today, where they want to be tomorrow, and how they plan to get there?

Are they being realistic? Ask for advice from professionals in a far-away market where you won't be in competition.

What three qualities should a veteran reading your chapter consider when choosing to venture into business?

A veteran should ask themselves the following questions: Do I have the work ethic to really do this? Do I have the resources to survive a tough first year? Have I done enough research? Am I prepared?

What would you say to a fellow veteran who is seeking to go into business for themselves?

Don't expect it to be easy. Don't get too excited about being your boss; you might not end up liking him. Be optimistic, but be realistic.

What sets you and your company apart from your competitors?

I believe that I go the extra mile for my customers. I make realistic promises, and then I exceed their expectations. I'm willing to take a loss rather than have bad word of mouth spread about me and my company.

About Bill Irwin

Company:

Data-Line Office Systems, Lubbock, Texas

How to Get in Touch with Me:

Website URL
www.datalinecentral.com

Email
billjr@datalinecentral.com

Phone Number
(806) 795-0658

CHAPTER ELEVEN

Putting Your Imagination to Work with Critical Thinking

Discussion with Ron Elsinger

Have you ever thought about putting your creative imagination to work with critical thinking and become successful? There are millions of entrepreneurs whose success today in business is standing tall because they were able to visualize their dream business ahead and fashioned it to become their vision. Ron Elsinger is such an entrepreneur! He is a U.S. Navy veteran who put his imagination to work with critical thinking to create his company long before retiring from the military as a Navy captain.

As a veteran about retiring, or entrepreneur-to-be, can you carve out the dream business you intend to own in the future like Ron Elsinger? How many veterans or would-be entrepreneurs can maximize their business skills with powerful critical thinking to achieve success like this outstanding entrepreneur? Ron Elsinger painted a vivid picture of how he can still make money by continuing with the same hypnosis services he rendered while in the Navy. He went ahead to treat pains, stress, weight, anger, mindfulness, and smoking issues for his clients after retirement to earn a living. With his vision to work with critical thinking, he has millions of clients, including certified registered nurses, doctors, and psychologists, teaching them throughout the States and many overseas countries.

One vital lesson every entrepreneur needs to learn from Ron Elsinger is that those who dare to put their imagination to work with critical thinking will end up having little or no obstacle standing in their way to success. As an entrepreneur-to-be, how much of your critical thinking is already at work to help move your business in the right direction? Read the story of Ron Elsinger and maximize your business potential by putting your imagination to work with critical thinking. As an entrepreneur who is determined to succeed, Ron Elsinger started his business at home, moved into one small office, and later into a larger building, which he eventually purchased. Who told you that with critical thinking, a business cannot start from the smallest office, school classroom, or in the hotel room until when there will be a better accommodation? Start to brainstorm and think critically like Ron, and you will have the future of your dream delivered earlier than thought.

Happy business voyage as you read his chapter!

Thank you so much for joining us today. Amongst many other areas of specialty, you are considered an expert in your field. Please tell us your full name, your professional title, and about your company.

I am Marco Ron Elsinger, and I am the owner of Healthy Relationships, a training company that does workshops and seminars. Most of our certified nurses are anesthetists. We are also the founders of the American Association of Moderate Sedation Nurses. We help people through hypnosis. We develop workshops and seminars, and we help people to do behavioral modification. So, we have a broad range of areas to help people create coping skills for everyday life health.

I use hypnosis or pain management for childbirth. We help in many different areas of the hospital setting, including weight management. As a matter of fact, we became so good at Naval Medical Center Report Smith that people with Phantom limb pain were brought to us.

Mention one big problem you specialize in solving.

Ron Elsinger: One of the big problems that I specialize in is chronic pain to get people to not have to go into opioids, become addicted. And I have worked with many people. One lady came to me; she had had pain for two years. I was addicted to opioids, and it was after she had had surgery for an abdominal hysterectomy. When she woke up from the surgery, she was in severe pain, which eventually got diagnosed as chronic cystitis. When we worked with her, we found out that it went right away. As soon as she realized why she had that pain, it never came back. That was amazing.

In the Navy, I put together a program. I teach all of our nurses working in areas that did sedation; I also taught the doctors basic safety procedures, helping them understand how to do simple things like knowing the right medication, how to do an assessment, know about airways, and all the things that would keep that patient safe. We are still the only ones doing this. We started it in 2004 after I retired. Hospitals seek my permission to use the program I have put together to teach their nurses. I made it a continuing education program. Then I added to it a certification, and we created our own association, American Association of Overstimulation Nurses. Now, we have a huge organization of nurses doing sedation that are not trained in anesthesia. So, that helped a lot in the process that we did.

Tell us why you think your business is important. What are the benefits of working with a company like yours?

Ron Elsinger: The vision that I created is important because, one, it fills a void; there is no other company that does it the way we do it. No other company offers continuing education credits and certification as our association. Our members also have access to conferences, free CE credits, and newsletters. So, what we do basically is, we develop the vet designs and market training mainly for nurses and hypnotist. And we focus on patient safety and teaching people how to overcome problems in their life by simply learning how to do mindfulness, meditation, guided imagery, being able to relax and get out of the stress causes, etc.

You do not need to have special licenses other than a business license to work with us, and that is a benefit. The training is readily available, in which we allow you to know exactly how to sit down and set up your business and to learn how to work with people. We organize a lot of active seminars and workshops so that you and your business can grow. The training is a step-by-step process—starting a business, building the foundation, and moving forward steadily.

What stirred you to move in this professional direction? Include a short story about how you caught the bug to do what you do. Describe what drives you and your passion to do what you do and to help others.

Ron Elsinger: I have done hypnosis through my entire NSSU year before I joined the Navy, I didn't join the Navy until I was 37 years old. I joined the Navy because when I went and asked how much money was in my retirement plan at the hospital, they told me I only had $25,009. I had been there for 11 years, so I knew that the reason that everybody working in Arizona in their seventies was that they couldn't afford to retire. I had been in the Army and the Marine Corps. When I wanted to join the Navy, I was told, "We can take you only if you are willing to drop a rank and a half, man." So I did, and that was the best decision, thanks to my wife who supported me in that. I became interested in hypnosis when I was working in pain clinics, where I helped patients to quit smoking using the right management skills. That became a key to my success.

Typically, how long does it take to recoup an investment in your business?

Ron Elsinger: First of all, you do not need to have any special education as far as degrees or special licenses to become a hypnotist. In the States, you cannot call yourself a hypnotherapist. Anybody can become a hypnotist. So, how much cash is it to invest where you need to take at least a certification course which can cost you from $500 up to $5,000? And then with that, you would need to have an office that can be shared with somebody else—for $250 or maybe even up to $1,500 a month.

It all depends on how much you are putting in. But for the initial, just get your certification as a hypnotist, find a place to do your hypnosis, and buy some literature or books so that you learn more about your profession. You can recoup easily within six months. If you are really good and know what you are doing, and you have a lot of people that you are networking with, you might be able to recoup it in two months. Again, it depends on how much you are willing to invest in your business; so, it's not a big deal. You do not have to go to college or have a degree or master's degree. You have to take a basic course and then start taking advanced courses. Then you start finding out what it is you are most interested in. Starting a business today is so simple and easy. All you need do is be willing to do the work that goes with it. You have to know what your resources are.

What resource have you used or had access to that you feel benefited you professionally to grow your business and is exclusive to veterans?

Ron Elsinger: Well, when we finally decided to quit renting or leasing and purchase our own building, we secured the veteran's loan at 2%, and that was a big deal for us. We got 40% of that loan at 2% interest rate, which was nice. The other is the P tag, which introduces you to government agencies, and when you get introduced to those government agencies, starting with the city, the county, the state, and even to the federal agencies, they can help you meet the people that would be purchasing your product. So, one of the big investments we made was being a veteran bent vendor and becoming AGSA and government contractors.

What misconceptions and fears have you had and have found that fellow veterans have about venturing into this line of Entrepreneurship and how did you resolve it?

Ron Elsinger: My misconception was, I could open my door, and people would automatically show up, and I thought did not need a website. I did not know what I wanted to do both in business and in moving out into the different communities that I would be teaching. Now, I teach sedation across the board for doctors and nurses, and I also teach hypnosis to nurses, doctors, psychologists, housewives, and even retired people.

And my fear in the beginning was, how long will it take me to replace my income? Then I made a decision while at an anesthesia conference. When I got back from the Buford Naval Hospital, where I was the director of patient services, I made a vow to retire from the Navy and go into business for myself. Now, the fears came not so much from me but from my wife because she was expecting me to make a decision. I shut the door to the Navy—and I did have a navy retirement—to do hypnosis full time, and that's how I started.

What tools and education did you receive during your military service career that helped you reach your level of success in business today?

Ron Elsinger: I have a diploma in nursing and anesthesia; the school was basically OJT (on-the-job training). So, the tool that I got from the military was working every day with people at the naval war college who were the best of the best, the elite of the elite; from how they paid attention to how they did things. I went in at age 37; I was older than everybody else basically at my rank, but I was always learning from the young people. When I attended a conference, I tried to find people who were brand new to the business to go see their perception of that business. How did they do their hypnosis? What did they do to become successful? I ask questions even from the youngest, least knowledgeable person there that is a hypnotist to see what their perception is of what they do. I never went there to tell them how to do stuff. I needed to know what other people were doing, especially if they were very experienced in the aspects of hypnosis.

Am I successful? Yes. I have seven employees, comprising part-time staff and contractors who work full time. We have a 5,000 square foot building, and my employees earn a very good income. I do not even pay myself that much. But what I do need is to see other people use our products and testify of how much it changed their lives—and we get that every day.

What do you think any veteran should know before deciding to venture into entrepreneurship?

Ron Elsinger: They need to know about the business and talk to somebody who is trained to guide and lead them. Someone who can help them with their critical thinking, help them put together a business plan, and balance their business and family. Do they have the money? Are they going to have to risk their personal assets? Are they self-starters, and can they plan and make decisions? Are they emotionally ready for the ups and downs or the stresses on their family, wife, kids, etc.?

Your business owns you, and only you know your skills, which means when you have the passion and hard work, then you have got the tenacity to stay at it. One of the hardest parts of that is when things are not going the way you want, but you have to stay enthusiastic and learn other skills as well so as to improve your business.

How can you help a veteran who is interested in business achieve the greatest success?

Ron Elsinger: What is your motivation and purpose? It is our desire, passion, belief and self-confidence that remains our driving force in business. You have to know everything about that type of business. You have got to find the experts. Google things you do not know or understand so you know what people are doing, how they got there, why they can build a business if it is a franchise. You need to find a way that fits your budget. I always work within a budget and the right business plan. So, go to the Chamber of Commerce; go to their meet and greets. Let people know who you are and what you do. Everybody meets a potential customer, no matter what you do.

Can you share an example of a project that you were able to work on and it became successful?

Ron Elsinger: We brought in a program of heart math so people could actually leave feedback to help us to find out what their baseline was. Through the program, we could actually show them how to take control of their anger and emotions. Well, that program actually ended up being a project that we took to the other middle schools within our county. We took the program of anger management, which anybody could have put together, and we did a pilot program for the middle school. From that pilot program, we did an anger management program for every school within Andy County, where we taught parents how to communicate with their children and teachers how to communicate with their students, and that was really a huge success for us.

Can you share a lesson you learned early in your career as a business leader that you overcame and now makes you the go-to person for your prospective clients?

Ron Elsinger: The biggest lesson that I learned was never to assume that you have got all the answers. My day starts with meditation; then I have a Ted talk. I have breakfast together with my staff, which I pay for, and then we take an hour to watch comedy and relax while eating together at lunch. So, I learned how to create a kind and stress-free environment and to have my projects done early. Believe in yourself and in your abilities. You have to lead yourself before you can lead others. Leadership does not come naturally, but management can be learned. Learn to manage and go to management classes.

What is the most important question veterans should ask themselves as they consider where they are today, where they want to be tomorrow, and how they plan to get there?

Ron Elsinger: "What am I willing to give up?" "What am I willing to spend?" "What am I willing to invest in order to start that business?" "How much free time would I have?" "Do I have what it takes to be an entrepreneur?" Those are the few questions you need to always have in mind so as to enable you have a focus and work toward your business goals and vision.

What three qualities should a veteran reading your chapter consider when choosing to venture into business?

Ron Elsinger: First of all, you have to be a critical thinker. You have to be open-minded and open to new ideas so you can always learn to improve your business. Secondly, you need to be hardworking and determined to get through the dark days. Be in search of new clients, and make efforts to meet clients' project deadlines. Lastly, you have to be willing to make sacrifices for your business, taking worthy risks so as to invest and grow.

What would you say to a fellow veteran who is seeking to go into business for themselves?

Ron Elsinger: Starting a business is like constructing a home; you have got to get all the paperwork done, all the permits signed. You have got to decide where you are going to build your home. You get to decide your community. So, you've got to build a foundation. The foundation is always the first part of the home. You may do your business full time or part-time. You need to ask yourself, "Should I be the business owner? Do I have the blueprints to get started?" Those are some of the things you have to consider before you decide to get into business.

What sets you and your company apart from your competitors?

Ron Elsinger: The thing that sets us apart is, we are innovators. We are always coming up with new ideas. We are always critically thinking about those things we have got and how we can make it better. The latest innovation that we have come up with came from one of the things that I would do with my clients after a hypnosis session—I would have them write down an affirmation to do at home, and then I would take that same affirmation, put it on a CD, put some music with it, and the next session, I would give it to them. Then I thought, *Is there any way thsey could put that on their phone?* So, we launched our new product. You can download our free app via Google or iTunes; nobody else has that. We have not gotten any competition after 12 years of putting that program forward. It was an innovative idea, but we took a risk. I took a risk when I hired somebody to put that program online, where people would watch the videos. We supplied the needed info, but the person we hired for the task got all the information, took it to their page, did their evaluation, did their certificate when we went out, etc. So, what we are doing now is really looking at the products that our competitors do not have that will generate us renewable income.

About Ron Elsinger

Company:

Healthy Relationships

Who can I help? We help businesses grow through the training, seminars, and workshops that we offer. We also help treat people who have any sort of chronic pain, stress, or anger through our management programs.

What sets me apart: We are an innovative company with critical and open-minded people who are always looking for new ways to improve and grow. We always come up with life-changing opportunities, and that is what sets me apart—my innovations and skills.

How to get in touch with us:

- Email
  RON@ESLINGER.NET
- Phone Number
  (865) 269-4616
- https://healthyvisions.com/

www.ingramcontent.com/pod-product-compliance
Lightning Source LLC
Chambersburg PA
CBHW021819170526
45157CB00007B/2647